The New York Times

PUBLIC PROFILES

Teen Activists

THE NEW YORK TIMES EDITORIAL STAFF

Published in 2020 by New York Times Educational Publishing
in association with The Rosen Publishing Group, Inc.
29 East 21st Street, New York, NY 10010

First Edition

The New York Times
Alex Ward: Editorial Director, Book Development
Phyllis Collazo: Photo Rights/Permissions Editor
Heidi Giovine: Administrative Manager

Rosen Publishing
Megan Kellerman: Managing Editor
Danielle Weiner: Editor
Greg Tucker: Creative Director
Brian Garvey: Art Director

Cataloging-in-Publication Data
Names: New York Times Company.
Title: Teen activists / edited by the New York Times editorial staff.
Description: New York : New York Times Educational Publishing,
2020. | Series: Public profiles | Includes glossary and index.
Identifiers: ISBN 9781642822540 (library bound) | ISBN
9781642822533 (pbk.) | ISBN 9781642822557 (ebook)
Subjects: LCSH: Youth—Political activity—Juvenile literature. |
Political activists—Juvenile literature. | Social action—Juvenile
literature.
Classification: LCC HQ799.2.P6 T446 2020 | DDC 320.40835—dc23

Manufactured in the United States of America

On the cover: On the anniversary of the Columbine shooting,
thousands of teenagers in New York City walked out of school to
attend a gun control rally and call for sweeping reforms in national
gun laws, April 20, 2018; Andrew Lichtenstein/Corbis News/Getty
Images.

Contents

CHAPTER 2

Parkland and the New Wave of Gun Control Activism

Introduction

THROUGHOUT THE HISTORY of the United States, activism has driven societal change. Young people have been at the heart of some of the most significant activist movements in the nation. While the efforts of college-age students have been largely recognized as important moments in the nation's history, the 21st century shines a spotlight on teenage activists.

Not yet old enough to vote, but politically involved and outspoken nonetheless, today's teenagers have plenty to fight for. As the 21st century heralds a new wave of teen activism, the tactics and tools available to activists have grown and changed. With passion and drive, coupled with a large reach of influence, today's teens may bring about a new era in the United States.

In the early 21st century, teenagers largely took up causes such as climate change, L.G.B.T.Q. rights and provincial issues such as their schools' dress codes. This generation of teenagers, also known as Generation Z, knows what kind of world they want to live in and they are ready to fight for it. However, in 2018, an incident occurred that no student should have to encounter: A gunman opened fire at the Marjory Stoneman Douglas High School in Parkland, Fla. He killed 17 people and wounded 17 others. It was the deadliest high school shooting in U.S. history.

After the Parkland shooting, much of teen activism was geared toward the gun control movement. Teenagers, who had previously sued their government over global warming and the right to protest the Pledge of Allegiance, began to lobby for stricter gun laws. While some adults tried to focus the conversation on mental health rather than gun control, teenagers demanded action.

Students from Marjory Stoneman Douglas High School joined hands with local activists during a rally in Greensboro, N.C., in August 2018. The rally was part of a nationwide tour to register voters and pursue stricter gun laws.

Through walkouts, marches, "die-ins," sit-ins, rallies and clapbacks on Twitter, teenagers proved to be informed and motivated. Several teens emerged as leaders of the gun control movement. Emma González, David Hogg and Sarah Chadwick, all of whom survived the Parkland shooting, became the faces of the cause. Emma González and David Hogg would become the most visible, enduring the most criticism and personal attacks, while Sarah Chadwick became known for her amusing and unapologetic action on Twitter.

While the activists may have been expecting opposition from lawmakers, they would also face the emotional burden of fighting for change after having experienced trauma and loss. Activism as a teenager is particularly challenging, as the journey from adolescence to adulthood is difficult in itself. The Parkland teenagers, and all teenage activists, must weigh their activism against their last years of childhood. Emma González and David Hogg both faced insults and threats. David Hogg was the victim of a swatting incident, during which someone called the police to his home to investigate a false claim. Teenagers on opposing sides of the gun control movement also faced challenges. Those not in favor of stricter gun laws found it difficult to speak up and navigate classrooms so heavily dominated by gun control activists.

The ultimate outcome of today's teenage activism is not yet clear. Whether change will occur in gun control or not, the issue is ingrained in the nation's identity: This is the largest teenage movement in the 21st century so far. Teenagers have carved out a space for themselves in a political and social conversation by defending their rights to life and liberty. As the tools of activism evolve and teen activists continue to be vocal about climate change, L.G.B.T.Q. rights, gun control and more, only time will tell how society will respond to the concerns of these young activists.

CHAPTER 1

From the Individual to the Collective

Teenagers in the United States are vocal on many issues. They protest high school dress codes. They reject obligations to participate in national anthems and pledges. They sue their government over climate change. They both protest, and fight for, the rights of L.G.B.T.Q. students. The teens of the 21st century do not always agree with each other, but they are motivated and well-equipped enough to generate buzz and, perhaps, to generate change for issues that affect individuals and society as a whole.

Baring Shoulders and Knees, Students Protest a Dress Code

BY AL BAKER | JUNE 6, 2012

THE FIRST HINT of the looming rebellion came from the lips of Hao Yang, 17, as he practiced ballroom dancing outside Stuyvesant High School on Wednesday morning, the first licks of sunlight casting a long shadow that made a perfect dance partner on the wall behind him.

"It's Slutty Wednesday," said Hao, a senior from Brooklyn, who is headed to Carnegie Mellon University to study electrical engineering.

"Today."

Within minutes, a demonstration materialized on West Street, in Lower Manhattan, opposite the entrance to Stuyvesant, one of New

"We're not coming in, like, naked," said Andreas Petrossiants, 17, left, with Gil Spivak, also 17. "This is acceptable to wear by society's standards."

York City's most prestigious public high schools: Scores of giddy students, who had mostly come up from the nearby subway portals, were massing under a tree.

Some peeled off sweatshirts, revealing tank tops and spaghetti-strap blouses. One boy stepped over to the tree's trunk, took off his pants and emerged in shorts whose hem he immediately began rolling up along his thigh.

Pieces of paper were dispersed, some bearing the message "Redress the Dress Code" typed in the center in small letters, others featuring a printout of the school's clothing guidelines, but with a big red "X" drawn through them.

What people were seeing, the students explained, was some steam being let off over their long-simmering discontent with a dress code Stuyvesant adopted last fall to combat some clothing styles the administration deemed unacceptable.

One rule says that any sayings and illustrations on clothing should be in "good taste." Another calls for shorts, dresses and skirts to extend at least beyond the fingertips when arms are extended straight down. A third bans the exposing of "shoulders, undergarments, midriffs and lower backs."

But the rules have been prompting waves of objections by students, particularly now that summerlike weather has arrived and, many noted, the school's air-conditioning has proved to be less than reliable.

Even before the protest on Wednesday, students had been listing their grievances in online forums and in The Spectator, the student newspaper, with many girls arguing that the rules, and the enforcement of them, were disproportionately aimed at them. They also complained about one solution that administrators had developed for offenders: making them wear oversize gray T-shirts.

"We're going to overpower the gray T-shirts," said Madeline Rivera, 18, a senior, before walking into the school. "We're outnumbering them now."

She said the rules seemed arbitrary, that staff members seemed to go after certain "body shapes," singling out girls whose bodies are "more curvy."

"It's a double standard," said Madeline, who wore a skirt that ended around her hanging wrists and a covered-up spaghetti-strap blouse, which she revealed shortly before entering the building. "I'm going to take this sweatshirt off and expose my shoulders."

Stuyvesant's principal, Stanley Teitel, declined to comment on the dress code policy or the protest, which involved several hundred of the school's 3,300 students. But students who participated said there had been no crackdown or mass distribution of T-shirts, suggesting that the school was just letting it play out.

A number of schools have dress codes, an Education Department spokeswoman, Marge Feinberg, said, noting that some even have uniforms. Valerie J. Reidy, the principal at the Bronx High School of

Students produced their own illustrated version of the dress code, complete with a red "X" to reflect their opinion of the rules.

Science, another elite school, said that there was a "pretty long" dress code at her school, and that it existed in written form for "at least 15 years, if not more."

On occasions that students break it, Ms. Reidy said, she has some spare clothes on hand — a T-shirt, a sweatshirt or pants. On Tuesday, she said, she had a senior turn his T-shirt inside out to conceal a logo she found offensive: a beer mug.

Outside Stuyvesant on Wednesday morning, the students, many of whom said they had their parents' support, offered rationales for their protest. "It's called Slutty Wednesday to symbolize that we're not actually slutty," said Benjamin Koatz, 18, a senior from Queens, whom many students credited with helping to organize the event via Facebook and other social media.

"That's the stigma, against wearing short-shorts," he added. "But actually, we're wearing what's comfortable."

Moments later, Benjamin jumped atop a concrete wall, with the boughs of the tree hanging above, and gave last-minute orders as if he were a field general before a military siege.

He said students should stick together if anyone was "pulled over." He suggested some answers they might give to the staff: "It's a comfort thing"; "In New York City, it is legal to be topless"; "I thought I'd dress a little more conservatively"; "I'm my own person, so deal with it."

Onward, the students went at 7:45 a.m., up over a footbridge that crosses West Street, toward the school's metal doors. Below them, on West Street, were adult joggers and mothers pushing baby strollers, some in provocative spandex or midriff-baring shorts and shirts.

The wooden planks of the bridge gave the scene a boardwalk feel.

"We're not coming in, like, naked," said Andreas Petrossiants, 17, who marched forth in a tank top and shorts. "This is acceptable to wear by society's standards."

One sophomore, Sweyn Venderbush, 16, said at lunchtime that he had mixed feelings about the protest.

"I don't know if what we're doing today is the right message to send," he said, questioning whether the protest's name furthered the cause, even if it was intended to be tongue in cheek.

Nonetheless, Sweyn, dressed in a preppy jacket and knee-length shorts, had joined in.

"I had my shorts rolled up for two periods," he said. "Better to participate in some way even if I don't totally agree."

Joel M. Winston, a technology teacher, said he believed that the clothing rules were not overly burdensome, adding that he thought some teachers could also dress better. Mr. Winston said culture, and parents, were to blame.

Despite the protest, he said he had seen many days when students, without an organized event, dressed more scantily.

"Today's better than most," he said.

ERIC P. NEWCOMER contributed reporting.

Missouri Teenagers Protest a Transgender Student's Use of the Girls' Bathroom

BY KAREN WORKMAN | SEPT. 1, 2015

A TRANSGENDER HIGH SCHOOL STUDENT in Missouri is facing backlash from her peers after requesting to use the girls' bathrooms and locker room.

More than 100 students at Hillsboro High School, about an hour south of St Louis, walked out of class on Monday in protest.

"I'm hoping this dies down," said Lila Perry, the 17-year-old who began identifying as a girl publicly in February. "I don't want my entire senior year to be like this."

Ms. Perry, who began feeling "more like a girl than a boy" when she was 13, said school officials gave her permission to use the girls' facilities as the new school year began.

The district's superintendent, Aaron D. Cornman, issued a statement saying the district "accepts all students no matter race, nationality/ethnicity, gender or sexual orientation."

The student protest came on the heels of a school board meeting on Thursday attended by so many parents it had to be moved to a bigger location.

"My goal is for the district and parents to have a policy discussion," said Derrick Good, a lawyer who has two daughters in the district and wants students to use either facilities based on their biological sex or other gender-neutral facilities.

He worked with the Alliance Defending Freedom, a Christian advocacy group, to draft a "student physical privacy policy" and submit it to the district, which has about 3,500 students.

Ms. Perry previously used a unisex faculty bathroom, the St. Louis Post-Dispatch reported.

Mr. Good said he got involved after hearing about a female student who encountered "an intact male" in the girls' locker room.

"It's a violation of my daughters' rights to privacy to not have a policy," he said.

The protesting students assembled outside the school for about two hours. Mr. Cornman said he did not believe any of them were penalized.

Ms. Perry, who dropped out of the physical education class that prompted her use of the girls' locker room, spent the two hours in her guidance counselor's office.

"I was concerned about my own safety," she said.

She said she knows of other, younger transgender students in the district and wants to open a dialogue so they have a better high school experience.

"It feels really awful that people are going to these extremes against me, not just in school but all over the Internet," Ms. Perry said. "But I've also received so much support. It feels really surreal to be in the middle of all of this."

The Missouri Gay-Straight Alliance Network will host a rally supporting Ms. Perry on Friday.

"I think that there are a lot of folks that don't understand the difference between sex and gender and only see Lila as her sex at birth," said Morgan Keenan, the group's founding director.

It's not the first case to stir public debate about the matter.

A 13-year-old transgender student at a junior high school in Idaho was given permission to use the girls' bathrooms earlier this year, prompting a parent to remove a student from the school, according to KBOI-TV.

Transgender Student in Bathroom Dispute Wins Court Ruling

BY MATT STEVENS | MAY 22, 2018

A FEDERAL JUDGE in Virginia has found in favor of a transgender student whose efforts to use the boys' bathrooms at his high school reached the Supreme Court and thrust him into the middle of a national debate about the rights of transgender students.

In an order handed down on Tuesday, Judge Arenda L. Wright Allen of the United States District Court for the Eastern District of Virginia denied a motion by the Gloucester County school board to dismiss the lawsuit brought by the student, Gavin Grimm.

The school board had maintained that Mr. Grimm's "biological gender" was female and had prohibited administrators from allowing him to use the boys' restrooms. He sued the school board in July 2015, alleging that its policy violated Title IX as well as the equal protection clause of the Constitution.

The board had argued in essence that its policy was valid because Title IX allows for claims only on the basis of sex, rather than gender identity, and that its policy did not violate the equal protection clause.

But Judge Wright Allen disagreed, writing that Mr. Grimm's transgender status constituted a claim of sex discrimination and that the bathroom policy had "subjected him to sex stereotyping," violations of the law.

"There were many other ways to protect privacy interests in a nondiscriminatory and more effective manner than barring Mr. Grimm from using the boys' restrooms," she continued. "The Board's argument that the policy did not discriminate against any one class of students is resoundingly unpersuasive."

In Tuesday's order, the judge directed lawyers for both parties to schedule a settlement conference within 30 days.

Gavin Grimm, in February 2017. His efforts to use the boys' bathrooms at his high school thrust him into the middle of a national debate about the rights of transgender students.

"I feel an incredible sense of relief," Mr. Grimm, now 19 and headed to college in the fall, said in a statement after the ruling. "After fighting this policy since I was 15 years old, I finally have a court decision saying that what the Gloucester County School Board did to me was wrong and it was against the law. I was determined not to give up because I didn't want any other student to have to suffer the same experience that I had to go through."

In a statement issued late Tuesday, the Gloucester County school board said it was "aware of the District Court's decision." It was not clear whether the board planned to appeal.

A spokeswoman for the Justice Department declined to comment on Judge Wright Allen's ruling on Tuesday.

One of Mr. Grimm's lawyers said Tuesday that he had moved to Berkeley, Calif., and would attend college in the Bay Area. The lawyer, Josh Block, said they were seeking nominal damages and a declaratory judgment that the bathroom policy violated Mr. Grimm's rights under Title IX.

"Title IX protects trans people, and that's what courts have been saying for years," said Mr. Block, a senior staff attorney with the A.C.L.U. who was the lead lawyer on Mr. Grimm's case. "Even though this administration wants to try to roll back protections, they can't change what the law says."

At issue in Mr. Grimm's case is whether Title IX, a provision in a 1972 law that bans discrimination "on the basis of sex" in schools that receive federal money, also bans discrimination based on gender identity. President Barack Obama concluded that it did.

But in February 2017, President Trump rejected the Obama administration's position and rescinded protections for transgender students that had allowed them to use bathrooms corresponding with their gender identity.

The practical effect of the Trump administration's change in position was limited, however, as a federal court had previously issued a nationwide injunction barring enforcement of the Obama administration's guidance.

Then, the next month, the Supreme Court announced that it would not decide whether Mr. Grimm could use the boys' bathroom at his high school. Although the court decided not to take his case at the time, some predicted that it would almost certainly return there eventually.

The March 2017 decision was a setback for transgender rights advocates, who had hoped the Supreme Court would aid their cause in much the same way it had helped same-sex marriage advocates two years before.

Instead, in a one-sentence order, the Supreme Court vacated an appeals court decision in favor of Mr. Grimm, and sent the case back to the federal appeals court in Virginia for further consideration in light of the new guidance from the Trump administration. The case was later returned to the District Court to consider whether the school district's policy had violated Mr. Grimm's rights.

Mr. Grimm's case is just one of several on transgender rights that have been litigated in lower courts or been the subject of federal civil rights investigations in recent years. In her order, Judge Wright Allen cited several cases with arguments similar to Mr. Grimm's. Even with Tuesday's federal order, there remains a thicket of conflicting state laws and local school policies on bathroom use.

Mr. Grimm's journey into the spotlight began in 2014, when he was 15 and starting his sophomore year. At that time his family told his school, Gloucester High School, that he was transgender. Administrators were supportive at first and allowed him to use the boys' bathroom.

But amid an uproar from some parents and students, the school board barred Mr. Grimm from using the boys' bathrooms and adopted a policy requiring students to use the bathrooms and locker rooms for their "corresponding biological genders." The board added that "students with gender identity issues" would be allowed to use private bathrooms.

The A.C.L.U. argued that requiring Mr. Grimm to use a private bathroom had been humiliating and had, quoting him, "turned him into 'a public spectacle' before the entire community, 'like a walking freak show.' "

In its statement, the school board said that it "continues to believe that its resolution of this complex matter fully considered the interests of all students and parents in the Gloucester County school system."

SHERYL GAY STOLBERG, ADAM LIPTAK and MATTHEW SEDACCA contributed reporting. DORIS BURKE contributed research.

Reaching Out to Younger Hearts and Minds About L.G.B.T.Q. People

BY SCOTT JAMES | JUNE 19, 2018

SAN FRANCISCO — The author M.G. Hennessey remembers the moment a few years ago, after reading a book with a disappointed 9-year-old. "He wished there was a book about a kid like him," she said.

The child was transgender, and although born female was living as a boy.

Ms. Hennessey decided she would write the book the child needed. "The Other Boy," published by HarperCollins for young readers, follows the life of Shane, a fictional transgender boy. Ms. Hennessey, who is heterosexual, hoped the book would enlighten children to be accepting of others.

"The more you see representations in the media, the more familiar it becomes," Ms. Hennessey said.

"The Other Boy" is part of a new battleground for rights for people who identify as lesbian, gay, bisexual, transgender or queer. As the L.G.B.T.Q. community has gained greater acceptance in America, some advocates now see an opportunity to prevent bigotry from taking root by reaching out to the youngest hearts and minds.

The fight is being waged in state legislatures and schools, but perhaps the most visible efforts are in the media, building on the "Will & Grace" effect, an acknowledgment that the TV sitcom has helped normalize L.G.B.T.Q. people as part of the nation's fabric.

Bringing gay-friendly messages to young children has faced opposition, and L.G.B.T.Q. advocates admit that gains have been tough to achieve in the current political climate.

At a glance, however, some recent L.G.B.T.Q. content for children has had such a high profile that one might think the rainbow flag had replaced the Stars and Stripes.

Perhaps the greatest recent success started as a joke. When the creative team at John Oliver's HBO TV show heard about a coming children's book about Vice President Mike Pence's real-life pet rabbit, it produced a parody titled, "Last Week Tonight With John Oliver Presents a Day in the Life of Marlon Bundo," published by Chronicle Books in March. In a jab at Mr. Pence's conservatism, the bunny in Mr. Oliver's version is gay, and he falls for another male rabbit and stumbles into a political ruckus.

Though introduced on a satirical adult show, the book was written with young readers in mind. To date, 800,000 copies have been published.

Natalie Ponte of Weston, Conn., read the book to her 4-year-old son, Milo, and wrote on Facebook that the experience was transformative.

"We are pretty open and progressive and this kid still had reservations at the beginning about two boy bunnies getting married," Ms.

From left, three books that have been in the spotlight for their takes on gender roles and sexuality: "Last Week Tonight With John Oliver Presents a Day in the Life of Marlon Bundo," a parody of a children's book; "The Other Boy," the story of Shane, a fictional transgender boy; and "It's Perfectly Normal," an illustrated guide to sexuality.

Ponte wrote. "After reading this book twice he was ready to run for office on a gay rights platform."

Other recent mainstream media efforts have reached huge audiences of children and families.

"Roseanne," the highest-rated television show of the season, featured a character who is a gender-nonconforming boy. And the "Star Wars" franchise introduced its first L.G.B.T.Q. character in "Solo: A Star Wars Story" — Lando Calrissian is pansexual, according to the writer Jonathan Kasdan.

Predictably, there has been criticism. Jim Daly, the president of Focus on the Family, a conservative Christian group that opposes gay rights, called Mr. Oliver's parody an attack on the vice president that was "vulgar and vile."

Slate magazine questioned whether the gender-nonconforming character on "Roseanne" was a cynical attempt to deflect from bigoted tendencies of the show's star, Roseanne Barr. The sitcom was canceled when Ms. Barr later posted a racist tweet.

And critics have pointed out that Mr. Calrissian's sexuality is not exhibited on screen, unless you count a flirtatious moment when he refers to Han Solo as "adorable."

But while Hollywood grabs the spotlight, a more lasting effort to reach children is underway at schools, with California in the forefront. This fall, California will be the first state where textbooks in primary schools will note when historical figures were L.G.B.T.Q. Additionally, the California Healthy Youth Act, amended in 2016, requires schools to offer sex education that includes information about sexual orientation and gender identities.

Deciding the details has divided some communities, as was the case in May in Fremont, Calif., a city of 233,000 residents on San Francisco Bay. Although near Silicon Valley in what many consider a liberal bubble, when the school board considered sex education for children as young as fourth grade, hundreds of agitated residents on both sides of the issue packed public meetings.

Sameer Jha, a 16-year-old activist from Fremont, Calif., has raised funds to buy L.G.B.T.Q. books for libraries. "Representation is important," Sameer said.

Some specifically objected to including the best-selling book "It's Perfectly Normal" by Robie H. Harris. The book, first published in 1994 with more than a million copies sold, is an illustrated guide to sexuality, updated recently to include gender identity.

"I've been called a tool of the gay agenda," Ms. Harris said in an interview. But she said that children had questions, and that her book answered them. "If it's in the best interest of the child, I'm going to put it in there."

Teri Topham, a French teacher at a local charter school whose own children attended the Fremont public schools, opposed the proposed curriculum as not age appropriate. She said the teachings conflicted with her Mormon beliefs, and she noted that the city has large Muslim and South Asian communities, some with conservative traditions.

"The public school system has to err on the side of caution," Ms. Topham said in an interview.

The school board rejected the proposed curriculum for the fourth and fifth grades.

The decision troubled Sameer Jha, 16, a Fremont resident who self-describes as "queer, still figuring it out, a gender flux."

Sameer said there was no mention of L.G.B.T.Q. people in fourth grade before. "All I knew was that it was a bad thing," Sameer said. Having since transferred to a "more inclusive" private school in Oakland, Sameer has become a public activist, helped Gay-Straight Alliance organizations and raised funds to buy L.G.B.T.Q. books for libraries.

"Representation is important," Sameer said.

While these and other efforts persist, life remains challenging for L.G.B.T.Q. youths, according to the Human Rights Campaign, a gay rights group that monitors cases of discrimination, bullying and harassment in schools.

"We have been responding to more fires than I have ever seen in K through 12," said Johanna Eager, an organization director. She said that since the election of President Trump, she had heard of "some of the most horrible hateful situations in schools that I have not experienced in the past almost 30 years."

Ms. Eager said that teacher training was needed, but that she also recognized the power of storytelling.

"If you really hear a compelling story about someone suffering as an L.G.B.T.Q. person," she said, "that can change someone's heart or mind quickly."

Even after the defeat in Fremont, Sameer saw opportunity. "We've made waves," Sameer said. "It's being talked about."

The Education of Amandla Stenberg

BY REGGIE UGWU | SEPT. 11, 2018

This 19-year-old actress and star of "The Hate U Give" has become synonymous with a volatile strain of youthful, social-media-fueled, hyper-progressive celebrity.

WEST HOLLYWOOD, CALIF. — There are roles certain actors seem born to play — an echo of facial symmetry, a rhyming of demeanor — and then there is Starr Carter, the high school junior of "The Hate U Give," and Amandla Stenberg, the young actress who seems to embody her almost from sense memory, as if the performance is actually self portraiture.

In a way, it is. Both Ms. Stenberg and her fictional counterpart shuttled between a lower-income black neighborhood and a wealthy white private school, beginning at the age of 10. Both were shaped by the mental gymnastics of traversing the two worlds, each of which seemed to require a distinct conception of self. And both were eventually jolted out of their youthful naïveté by the same grimly modern rite of passage — the killing of an unarmed black man at the hands of a white police officer.

In the novel on which the film is based, which dramatizes some of the events that galvanized the Black Lives Matter movement, Starr's seamless shifting between identities, or code switching, masks an internal sense of isolation and chaos that particularly moved Ms. Stenberg, 19, who grew up in black and Latino South Los Angeles and attended school in a white Westside neighborhood.

"There was this barrier that was always going to prevent me from being a part of that community in the same way that those kids were," she recalled in a recent interview. "I learned to be silent about certain factors of my life, like struggles with money. While other kids talked about all the things they did and places they traveled over summer break, my friends and I mostly kept to ourselves."

The actress says her activism "creates this impression of seriousness or that I won't make mistakes, and that's daunting, because I'm not always serious, and of course I'll make mistakes."

Ms. Stenberg spoke over walnut shrimp at a West Hollywood Chinese restaurant and hole-in-the-wall music venue — an old haunt. Her hair was a bouquet of black phone-cord curls that she swept to one side, and she was wearing a houndstooth jumpsuit, its neutral tone framed by the blare of the restaurant's fire-engine-red leather banquettes.

She is the beating heart and battered soul of "The Hate U Give," a searing and timely family drama and coming-of-age story, in theaters Oct. 19, that trails the toppled dominoes of systemic racism in a nominally integrated fictional town.

Like other socially minded films this year, including "BlacKkKlansman" and "Blindspotting," "The Hate U Give" sees raw material in the magma of still-smoldering news headlines and social media hashtags. But Ms. Stenberg's star turn does the most critical load bearing, somehow channeling an emerging generation's inchoate rage, grief and resilience into one recognizably human form.

"She has this ability to make you feel like you're seeing the real deal, which comes from a level of dedication to the material that's rare at any age," the film's director, George Tillman Jr., said in a phone interview. "I was already excited by the work I'd seen from her, but it's even more exciting to think about the work she's yet to do."

Ms. Stenberg, who graduated from high school only last year, has been acting nearly her entire life, a fact she attributes to a childhood spent in a community where auditions were a standard-issue extracurricular activity, alongside tap dancing and gymnastics. She landed her first acting gig at 5, as a blurry but effusive girl in the background of a doll commercial. By 12, she had appeared in her first film, playing a young Zoe Saldana in the 2011 action thriller "Colombiana." A role the next year in "The Hunger Games," as Rue, the plucky and diminutive ally to Jennifer Lawrence's Katniss Everdeen, put her on the map.

"The Hunger Games" was an early education in both the boon of celebrity and its hazards. Even as critics praised her performance,

Ms. Stenberg, whose mother is African-American and father is Danish, became the subject of a now familiar strain of racist internet backlash, in which some fans of the novel noxiously objected to the casting of a person of color. (Rue is described in the original novel as having "dark brown skin.") It was her first encounter with explicit racism, an experience that, along with more subtle displays of prejudice at her private school in Los Angeles, shaded her perception of hidden forces in society.

"I felt alone in it, or isolated by it," she said. "It made me feel like it was better to become smaller, or quieter, or less obtrusive or something."

In 2014, she was an incoming high school junior during the summer Michael Brown was shot and killed by a police officer in Ferguson, Mo. Shortly before, Eric Garner had died in a violent encounter with the police in New York City, and the resulting cascade of protests, demanding police reform and calling out racial injustice, clanged in her head like an alarm.

"Recognizing those events for what they were and seeing everyone make the choice to stand up against it completely informed what I cared about and what I felt my point was as an artist," she said. "It made me feel like I could do something, or, at least try to inform people."

For a project in her modern American history class that year, she and a classmate had to trace the history of an American artifact over a decade. They chose cornrows, the traditional African-American hairstyle, which had been the subject of a recent Marie Claire article hailing Kendall Jenner as a pioneer.

In Ms. Stenberg's finished project, a video titled "Don't Cash Crop My Cornrows," she contrasted the celebration of black cultural products with the denigration of black bodies. Some of her white classmates gave it a cool welcome. "They thought it was unfair and in some ways attacked white people," she said.

But, a few months later, she posted the video on her Tumblr account, where it quickly went viral.

BuzzFeed called it "the realest explanation of cultural appropriation." NBC News said it was "an authoritative history lesson on black culture." Ms. Stenberg, who speaks in scrupulous, quasi-academic paragraphs, continued to use her social media as a megaphone, especially in defense of Black Lives Matter, or to denounce what she saw as the collateral indignities of the patriarchy. After the 2016 election (a photo of her perched on a street sign at the Women's March made headlines), she wrote to her nearly two million followers on Instagram that President Trump's victory was "evidence that we are rapidly shifting the narrative, changing our cultural climate, and demanding equality — and that is a terrifying and immediate threat to white privilege."

Time magazine twice selected her as one of the most influential teenagers in the world; she was cheered by such feminist matriarchs as Oprah, Gloria Steinem and Beyoncé; and Ms. Stenberg, along with friends and fellow actresses like Rowan Blanchard, Yara Shahidi and Zendaya, became synonymous with a genus of progressive young celebrities whose incipient fame was as much a product of dexterous social advocacy as red carpet appearances or box office receipts.

At the Chinese restaurant in West Hollywood, she excused herself from a photo shoot to take a phone call from her agent. He was excited by a sponsorship offer from a large fashion company, she said later, and urged her to consider "a great opportunity." But Ms. Stenberg had dismissed the offer out of principle.

"I feel like fashion is kind of the epitome of a white institution that you have to mold yourself in order to fit into," she said. "I'm less interested in doing that now."

For a six-month period in 2017, during which she filmed both "The Hate U Give" and "The Darkest Minds," a "Hunger Games"-esque young adult fantasy film released in August, she gave up her iPhone for an antiquated Samsung slider and stepped back from social media. She hadn't liked the effect that constant connection was having on her brain. Her thoughts seemed to be "constantly buzzing around and not really landing anywhere." And at night, between the time she put down her phone and fell asleep, she felt a twitchy sense of chaos in the darkness.

Her online experience at the time had chafed, as well. Seemingly every day, torrid brush fires in the post-Trump culture war, or, more grievously, life or death miscarriages of criminal justice, materialized in her feeds. Because of her reputation, Ms. Stenberg had felt as if her followers expected her to contribute to each uproar, with note-perfect nuance and indignation. Her social media accounts, once tools of self-discovery and free expression, had become like chains of her own design.

"There was this precedent for how people expected me to act on the internet, this image that I'm supposed to fulfill," she said. "People think of me as a revolutionary or someone who is very inclined toward activism, and although activism is the driving force behind all of my work, it creates this impression of seriousness or that I won't make mistakes, and that's daunting, because I'm not always serious, and of course I'll make mistakes."

The smartphone hiatus ended in January — the lack of reliable mobile email proved terminal — and she's resumed posting regularly to her accounts. But the composition of the posts has changed. Ms. Stenberg now largely uses her Instagram for more lighthearted content ("I'm slowly turning it into a meme account," she joked) or to fulfill work and social obligations, of which there is no shortage.

" 'Why don't you post pictures of me? Why don't you post a photo from this shoot? Did she post a video of the teaser that we just made?' " she said, parroting a few common requests. Recently, she self-mockingly renamed her account "amandlasponsored." "It all feels kind of absurd to me," she said.

A few personal pictures still remain, including some of her girlfriend, the ascendant pop singer-songwriter Mikaela Straus, who records under the name King Princess. The two met at a music industry party (in addition to acting, Ms. Stenberg sings and plays multiple instruments) and quickly bonded.

Though she had come out as bisexual at 17, Ms. Stenberg announced that she was gay in a June interview in Wonderland magazine, for which Ms. Straus served as interlocutor. "I was so overcome with this profound sense of relief when I realized that I'm gay — not bi, not pan, but gay — with a romantic love for women," she said at the time.

Some criticized her shifting conception of her sexuality as evidence of phoniness. In our interview, Ms. Stenberg said she had simply wanted to be transparent about her journey, both for her own peace of mind and for the sake of others going through similar experiences. But she added that her words shouldn't be taken as written in stone.

"Will I change? Could my ideas about who I am and my sexuality and gender shift in the future? Very much so. It's very likely that it could. And I think that's O.K.," she said. "I'm not tied to the idea that everything I say has to be given so much weight. But I hope that it makes people feel less alone."

These days, Ms. Stenberg wants people to judge her for the work she does onscreen. That, too, is another plank of her activism, one she is approaching with characteristic intentionality. She accepted her role in "The Darkest Minds," she said, to "infiltrate systems that have traditionally been owned by white people." And she can currently be seen in "Where Hands Touch," a provocative, 1940s love story about a young biracial woman and a member of the Hitler Youth. (It was preceded by its own brush fire, with some commenters online objecting to the idea of a Nazi romance.)

By unifying her creative and political ambitions, Ms. Stenberg has fueled the potential for both self-expression and self-exposure. That the two are inextricable can be bruising. But it can also be a source of strength.

"I hope I always make work that is reflective of what I believe in," she said. "If art isn't personal, then it doesn't speak to me."

High School Students Explain Why They Protest Anthems and Pledges

BY VALERIYA SAFRONOVA AND JOANNA NIKAS | OCT. 21, 2017

Colin Kaepernick's decision to sit or take a knee during the national anthem exploded into a national conversation about race. Here, high school students tell us why they sit or kneel during the national anthem or the Pledge of Allegiance — or why they stand and participate.

IN AUGUST 2016, the National Football League quarterback Colin Kaepernick began sitting, and then kneeling, during the national anthem before games as a protest against racist treatment of black people in the United States. His gestures created a new front in the national conversation about race, policing and patriotism.

His action spread beyond the N.F.L., to soccer fields and basketball courts, and into high schools across the country. In recent weeks, as more players in the N.F.L. have locked arms, taken a knee or raised their fists during the national anthem, some students have again taken similar actions.

We asked high school students to tell us why they sit or kneel during the national anthem or Pledge of Allegiance, or why they stand and recite the words. Here is what they had to say.

NAYLAH WILLIAMS, 17
New York
Knelt during football games this year

My first reaction to seeing Colin Kaepernick kneeling was: Why did he do this? And what does it mean to him? I Googled it, I looked on social media, I talked to my parents. One thing my mom said to me is that I wouldn't be thinking about this so much if it didn't mean a lot to me. It was bothering me that I was thinking about not kneeling because it's one of those things where I can't sit back and watch everything happen and not say something about it.

In school, we learn about America and why things are the way they are. To take a step back and look at how things are, you can see that something doesn't add up. The America we learn about in school is about justice and the fundamental rights that this country is built on, including that everyone has the same rights. That's not happening. People from different races have fought for different rights, and people are not giving them those rights.

There was one football player that approached a few other cheerleaders and me. He told me this is what they wanted to do and why they wanted to do it. I wanted to make sure they weren't doing it just to follow what N.F.L. players did. **I wanted people to see that there is social injustice, racial inequality and police brutality.** I didn't want people to use that as an excuse to make a name for themselves. I wanted them to kneel because they felt in their heart that was the right thing to do.

I was definitely nervous. It's not easy standing up for something that could cause so much controversy, but when you know it's right, it makes it easier. Some people were supportive. This one lady came up to me and said I was so inspirational and that she wanted a picture with me. Another lady dropped off flowers for me at school.

There was a lot of hate that went around. Some of the football players received death threats and people saying it was disrespectful to kneel. It went around a lot more than we anticipated. So many other people were posting it. It was getting hundreds of thousands of likes, so a lot of people had a lot to say. The football players were scared. I was scared. We didn't expect it to get so big, and we didn't know how to handle it.

The second game I knelt at, there were people in the parking lot with a Confederate flag. It was nauseating. Not many people show up to the games. Going out to the stands and seeing all these people show up, I realized this is bigger than I thought it was going to be. I feel that with time, people will understand. Changing someone's view on something isn't easy to do.

I'm happy with it. I'm proud of myself for standing up for something

I believe in, even if other people don't. The people who know why I did it, I want them to know they're not alone. It's a lot scarier to do something by yourself than when you have people doing it with you.

TRENTON FAULKNER, 18
Texas
Always stands for the national anthem

I really choose to stand to show respect to everyone who is in service, who is on duty at the moment. They give so much and they get so little. The national anthem, the pledge, it's all showing respect to people doing their duty overseas in order for us to have the freedom to protest.

My dad and my brother both served in the army, and I'm trying to go into the Navy SEALs. People coming back from the war and facing personal issues, this probably makes them feel so low.

I know it's a right whether or not to stand or sit, but overall it's showing respect to people who are fighting for us. We hardly ever give them anything back. These football players get paid millions of dollars a day to sit on a bench. People who are fighting wars get paid $26,000 a year.

I think the kids kneeling in high schools are following a trend. There are only a few who will actually dedicate their time to this subject. All the kids like to follow the trends. They probably don't really reason with what they're doing. They feel like it's cool to follow along.

It's an O.K. thing to recognize an issue with race. Some people complain they're not getting paid as much as someone else or that they're getting treated wrong because of their race. **Maybe the right place to really protest would be D.C. Doing a peaceful march and doing speeches in Washington would be the most beneficial plan for them.**

JAHMIRE CASSANOVA, 17
New York
Knelt during games this year and last year

At our homecoming in October, one other person in my grade, a person in the grade above me, and I decided to kneel for the national anthem.

That was the only time we had the anthem before the game. We all identify as black males. It was a bit interesting that we were the only ones who did it.

A couple of days earlier we had been talking about kneeling for the anthem. **It was a natural conversation we were having in response to all the things going on with Colin Kaepernick. Growing up as a black male, and not adhering to stereotypes of what a black male in the U.S. could be, I've always been very sensitive to acts that lack equity in the population of black males.**

My parents always had conversations about how I should conduct myself based on real-life violence that occurs and based on stereotypes. Would I come home late? Would I take the subway? It has always been an uneasy thing for me to handle, especially when I was younger. **It's a discomfiting feeling to always have to present yourself a certain way, especially when you know the type of person you are and the goals you're setting for yourself.** As I got older, I realized how you are doesn't matter as much as it should because other individuals can't tell those things just by looking at you.

When I knelt, on the one hand I felt connected to people who protest against racial inequality and discrimination, but at the same time I felt a disconnect from a number of people in the community at Horace Mann. Not because they weren't kneeling but because I was, and I wasn't sure if they shared the same sentiments I do about racial discrimination.

ELLIE VAHEY, 16
Ohio
Knelt during soccer games

A teammate approached me about the idea to take a knee in order to show solidarity with victims in our country of violence and oppression, specifically minorities. **We obviously don't have the platform that professional athletes do. We knew this wouldn't solve the problem, but we thought it would be a good way to evoke conversation and get people in our community to confront what has been going on in the news.**

The first time, there were eight of us. It's been that number consistently. We've done it at three games.

We wrote an email to the athletic director in our school on behalf of three of us who had interest. We weren't asking for permission since it's a constitutional right, but we wanted to keep everybody on the same page.

Since our team is almost all white, some people felt that taking a knee wasn't the best way to solve the problem or to protest. When you see someone white taking a knee, it can be almost like, "Oh, they don't have anything to complain about. Why are they taking a knee?"

But the message we wanted to send is solidarity with minorities who face violence at the hands of police officers in our country. Because of my race and how I was born, I was born into a position of privilege. I felt like I have a moral obligation to do something and not be silent. There are situations where you can't be a bystander. It's important to make a gesture and raise your voice, even if that voice is a small one.

In America one of the most beautiful things is we have the right to express our opinions how we want to. If people are feeling obligated to stand for the national anthem, I think that's a very big red flag. Because America is not the land of the free for everyone in our country, I think that people should have the right to see America both for its accomplishments but also for its flaws. For a coach to tell a player not to take a knee, that goes against everything our country stands for and the rights that the brave men and women that serve this country fight for.

EMMA COWAN, 17
New York
Has not stood for the Pledge of Allegiance in school consistently for two years

It was about two years ago that I stopped saying it every day. I'm a senior in high school. In 10th grade, I wouldn't say it, but I would stand up. **Now as my own silent protest, I sit during the Pledge of Allegiance.**

I have no connection to religion whatsoever. The fact that they added the "under God" part to the Pledge of Allegiance doesn't represent me, and it doesn't represent others who do not have religious affiliations.

I definitely support the reasons that Colin Kaepernick keeps referring to. The tension between the police and African-Americans is not being resolved in a way that is benefiting the African-American community. The police system is not being altered in a way that will make it not inherently racist and allow it to protect every individual regardless of color. What I'm upset by is a coach saying, "I will bench someone who takes a knee." That's an injustice because you can't exercise your freedom of speech by doing a silent, personal protest.

There are things you can do besides saying the pledge to show that you support this country even if it might not support you. My mom is a public-school teacher. For her, it's helping others get a public-school education. For me, it's standing up for the rights that the country has promised to protect — I went to the Women's March in Washington, D.C.

CAROLINE SLACK, 17
Virginia
Stands for the Pledge of Allegiance but shows her opinion in other ways

I saw the news when Colin Kaepernick kneeled. But nothing ever really came up at my high school physically for a while. Most of the time the protests happen during the Pledge of Allegiance. For example, after the presidential election a lot of people I knew were considering staying seated during the Pledge of Allegiance. If you are sitting, they know what you're standing for or against.

I stand because I have family who is in the military, and I have a lot of reasons why I would stand for the flag. But I don't put my hand over my heart because while I do stand for the United States, I know that there are there are issues that need to be addressed. Issues that I will not personally face because I am a white girl in the South in a middle-class family. So when taking my hand off my heart, it's my way of acknowledging that there's something happening. But it's a kind of a quieter way of showing my opinion.

I don't want to be someone who stands by and watches it. I want to be active. It's hard to be active just standing or sitting. **I think that when I get into college I'll be able to be more public about my beliefs and my opinions. But for now leaving my hand off my heart kind of shows that there is something wrong with what's happening.**

A.J. CABRERA
Illinois
Took a knee alongside her dance team at a football game

Before the national anthem, my whole dance team took a knee, as well as the football team and the cheerleading team. And my own superintendent came up and gave a speech about microaggressions and racial hatred among our communities and in this country. He wanted to make it clear that bigotry wasn't tolerated at the school. And he wanted to make it clear that we were all in it together.

The kneeling was something that we talked about during the week. **With my team, we had to make it clear that it wasn't just a trend,** we weren't doing it just because the cheerleading squad was doing it or because the football players were. But because we actually wanted to take a stand for what we believed in.

I took a knee because I feel that to stand for the flag is to agree that it is a symbol of freedom and justice. For me, to stand for the anthem and to put my hand on my heart feels a bit ironic considering the fact that we are not living an American dream. There are so many things wrong that we still need to fix and address.

I think that while racism is erased from the laws, women have rights and the laws prohibit racial bigotry, that doesn't mean it is not abundant in society. You can still see very clear examples of this when you read the news. For example, if you look at the Las Vegas shooter, who was white, most of the headlines I see describe the shooter as the "least expected to do this," or "he was a humble man," or "he was a nice neighbor." But shooters of other races immediately get the label of what they are, these people are terrorists, these people are murderers. While this man, who caused one of the worst mass shootings in U.S. history, is given a humane perspective.

When I was taking a knee and I saw everyone else joining us in the action of taking a knee, **I just felt really powerful and united with everyone at my school. I felt really proud of my community and how we had all come together.**

2 Texas Students Sue Schools to Freely Protest the Pledge

BY NIRAJ CHOKSHI | OCT. 30, 2017

LONG BEFORE PRESIDENT Trump escalated the debate over protests during the national anthem, two Texas teenagers began challenging injustice in their own way, by sitting through the recitation of the Pledge of Allegiance.

Now, they are separately suing their schools, saying that teachers and administrators shamed or punished them for their protests, violating their constitutional rights. The students, both in the Houston area, said they had received especially harsh treatment in recent months.

One school district denied the claims, and the other said it would not comment on any potential litigation.

"It just seems that there is something in the air," said Randall Kallinen, a civil rights lawyer in Houston who is representing the students, who are both 17.

The president may have played a role. Last month, Mr. Trump ignited a heated national debate over the decision by some N.F.L. players to kneel during the national anthem to protest against racial injustice.

Like those athletes, the Texas students, India Landry and another teenager, identified only by her initials, M.O., said their protests stemmed from a sense that the nation had failed to uphold the promise of the pledge.

"We live in a country where there isn't justice and freedom for all, and so I'm not going to stand for a pledge that says there is," the student whose name was withheld said at a news conference last Wednesday.

That teenager, a senior at Klein Oak High School outside of Houston, began her protest when she started high school in 2014, according to a lawsuit filed in federal court last week against nine school and district officials and the district itself.

Over the years, teachers and students criticized her for refusing to stand, and administrators ignored or defended the harassment, according to the teenager and her mother, LaShan Arceneaux.

At one point, a guidance counselor suggested that the student switch out of a journalism class whose teacher had insisted she stand, according to the lawsuit. This year, a teacher told the teenager's class that those who sat through the pledge were comparable to Soviet communists, pedophiles and Islamist extremists, the lawsuit said. Classmates harassed the teenager online and in person, including as recently as last week, Mr. Kallinen said.

Because of the harassment, Ms. Arceneaux decided in the spring to home-school her daughter before allowing her to return to school in August, according to the suit. The teenager, who said on Wednesday that she had a 3.9 G.P.A., continued to participate in debate competitions while being home-schooled, but at an expense of more than $10,000 to the family, according to the suit.

In a statement, the Klein Independent School District disputed the accusations.

"Klein I.S.D. denies the allegations and, after investigation and discussion with those involved over a three-year span, finds multiple discrepancies in the allegations," the statement said. The district added that it respected the rights of its students and "does not tolerate harassment" against them.

Ms. Arceneaux said her daughter made the decision to protest the pledge on her own, but added that she understood the reasoning.

"Obviously in this country I can see there's not liberty and justice for all," Ms. Arceneaux said at the news conference. "I'm still an African-American woman in this country, and I can see the news and things that go on around me."

The lawsuit is funded by American Atheists, a nonprofit that fights for the separation of church and state and has helped students with similar disputes. It joined the effort after Ms. Arceneaux and her daughter reached out, a spokesman said. Neither the teenager nor her mother is an atheist, Mr. Kallinen said.

The Supreme Court weighed in on the issue decades ago, ruling in a 1943 case, West Virginia State Board of Education v. Barnette, that requiring students in public schools to salute the flag or recite the Pledge of Allegiance amounts to a violation of their First Amendment rights.

This month, Mr. Kallinen filed a similar lawsuit on behalf of another mother and her daughter, Kizzy and India Landry. That suit was filed in federal court against the Cypress-Fairbanks Independent School District and Martha Strother, the principal at Windfern High School in Houston, which India attends.

India's protest against injustice began about a year and a half ago and was tolerated by at least half a dozen teachers until this month, according to the lawsuit.

On the morning of Oct. 2, India was with Ms. Strother and a school secretary in the principal's office, according to the lawsuit. When the pledge was recited over the school speakers, both women stood. Ms. Strother asked India to join them and expelled her when she refused, the lawsuit said.

"She asked me to, and I said I wouldn't," India told KHOU, a local television news station. "And she said 'Well, you're kicked out of here.' "

India was sent to an assistant principal who instructed her to call her mother for a ride home, warning that Ms. Landry had five minutes to arrive or India would be escorted away by the police, according to the lawsuit. "This is not the N.F.L.," the secretary reportedly said.

When Ms. Landry arrived, she was told that Ms. Strother would not see her, according to the suit. At a meeting several days later, Ms. Strother said India could not return to school until she agreed to stand for the pledge, the lawsuit said. The KHOU segment aired that afternoon and, the next day, Ms. Strother reversed course.

In a statement provided to The Times on Friday, the school district said it had not been served with documentation regarding the lawsuit and would not comment on litigation. India is back in school, the statement said.

In both lawsuits, Mr. Kallinen said the schools had violated his clients' First, Fifth and 14th Amendment rights.

The East L.A. Walkouts, 50 Years Later

BY TIM ARANGO AND MATT STEVENS | MARCH 6, 2018

FIFTY YEARS AGO this month, amid the tumult of the 1960s, thousands of Chicano students from Los Angeles high schools walked out of class to protest racism and failing schools.

"I was pretty beat down," recalled Bobby Verdugo, who was one of the student organizers. "I didn't think I would amount to much. That's what teachers were telling me."

As Mr. Verdugo, 67, and other veterans of the Chicano walkouts made the rounds of events at schools here recently, to mark the anniversary, students told them about their own intentions to walk out of class next week, in solidarity with student activists across the country who have called for protests for gun control in the aftermath of the shooting in Parkland, Fla.

"I couldn't help but reflect back," he said. "Before us, high school kids had never done that en masse."

With the gun protests planned for next week, on March 14, commentators have invoked the historic parallels to the 1960s, when students protested against the Vietnam War and in favor of civil rights. The history of his own movement, Mr. Verdugo said, is often forgotten.

Writing in The Los Angeles Times recently, Gustavo Arellano, a columnist, said: "Those young people helped launch the Chicano movement in Southern California and created a generation of leaders."

Mr. Arellano worries that the national news media coverage of the Parkland-inspired activists will ignore the Chicano walkouts, and focus instead on the youth movements against the Vietnam War and segregation in the South, and more recent youth-led protests against President Trump's immigration policies.

But in Los Angeles this week no one is ignoring that history. Los Angeles schools have held a number of events, including a reenactment on Monday of a famous meeting in 1968 between Cesar Chavez, the Chicano labor leader, and Robert F. Kennedy.

"Chicano history was not separate from American history, it was a part of American history," Mr. Verdugo said.

One of the sparks for the protests here in 1968 was a high drop-out rate among Latino students. And Mr. Verdugo, who was failing in school, left for good after the protests. But later that year he was admitted to U.C.L.A. under an affirmative action program.

"I walked out in March, dropped out in May, and in October I walked on to the campus of U.C.L.A.," he said.

He never graduated, but years later earned a degree from another university and went on to a long career in social work.

Are Civics Lessons a Constitutional Right? This Student Is Suing for Them

BY DANA GOLDSTEIN | NOV. 28, 2018

Many see the lack of civics in schools as a national crisis. A federal lawsuit says it also violates the law.

ALEITA COOK, 17, HAS NEVER taken a class in government, civics or economics. In the two social studies classes she took in her four years at a technical high school in Providence, R.I. — one in American history, the other in world history — she learned mostly about wars, she said.

Left unanswered were many practical questions she had about modern citizenship, from how to vote to "what the point of taxes are." As for politics, she said, "What is a Democrat, a Republican, an independent? Those things I had to figure out myself."

Now she and other Rhode Island public school students and parents are filing a federal lawsuit against the state on Thursday, arguing that failing to prepare children for citizenship violates their rights under the United States Constitution.

They say the state has not equipped all of its students with the skills to "function productively as civic participants" capable of voting, serving on a jury and understanding the nation's political and economic life.

The state allows local school districts to decide for themselves whether and how to teach civics, and the lawsuit says that leads to big discrepancies. Students in affluent towns often have access to a rich curriculum and a range of extracurricular activities, like debate teams and field trips to the State Legislature, that are beyond the reach of poorer schools.

The lawyers for the plaintiffs hope the case will have implications far beyond Rhode Island, and potentially prompt the Supreme Court to reconsider its 45-year-old ruling that equal access to a quality education is not a constitutionally guaranteed right.

TONY LUONG FOR THE NEW YORK TIMES

"I don't know what I'm supposed to know," said Aleita Cook, 17, one of the students who are suing Rhode Island, saying the state violated their constitutional rights by failing to prepare them for citizenship.

"Our real hope for reinvigorating our democratic institutions comes with the young people and the next generation," said Michael Rebell, the lead lawyer for the plaintiffs and executive director of the Campaign for Educational Equity at Teachers College, Columbia University. "What we're really seeking is for the courts, especially the Supreme Court, to take a strong stance on getting back to first principles on what the school system was established for in the United States."

Horace Mann, an early advocate of compulsory public schooling, wrote in 1847 that education's purpose was to foster "conscientious jurors, true witnesses, incorruptible voters."

More recently, the retired Supreme Court justices Sandra Day O'Connor and David Souter have called for a revival of civic instruction. Since the election of President Trump, politicians from both parties have proposed civics lessons as a way to combat political ignorance and division.

The case is riding a wave of bipartisan anxiety about a national lack of civic engagement and knowledge, from voter participation rates that are among the lowest in the developed world to pervasive disinformation on social media.

Fewer than half the states hold schools accountable for teaching civics, according to a review in 2016 by the Education Commission of the States. Only 23 percent of American eighth graders were proficient in civics on the 2014 National Assessment of Educational Progress, a test that included questions on the Constitution and the roles of the various branches of government.

Rhode Island does not require schools to offer courses in government or civics, does not require standardized tests in those subjects or in history, and does not provide training for teachers in civics, the lawsuit says.

Beyond civics classes, the suit also argues that the state's neediest children, particularly Latino immigrants and students with special needs, are failing to acquire the basic academic skills they need to effectively exercise their rights to free speech and voter participation.

Among eighth grade English-language learners in 39 states, those in Rhode Island ranked last in math and second to last in reading on the 2017 National Assessment of Educational Progress.

The Rhode Island Department of Education declined to comment on the allegations in the suit.

The argument Aleita's lawyers are making will be a heavy legal lift, as federal courts have, for four decades, been hostile to education inequality claims.

In the 1973 case San Antonio v. Rodriguez, the Supreme Court ruled 5 to 4 that the State of Texas had not violated the equal protection clause of the 14th Amendment by funding schools in low-income neighborhoods at lower levels than schools in more affluent areas. In July, a federal judge in Michigan declined to challenge that precedent, ruling that "access to literacy" was not a constitutional right for schoolchildren in Detroit.

The plaintiffs' lawyers in the Rhode Island case believe that, by focusing on civics, they can take advantage of an opening in the Rodriguez ruling. Justice Lewis F. Powell, writing for the majority, agreed with a dissenter in the case, Justice Thurgood Marshall, that educational inequality might rise to the level of a constitutional violation if it prevented students from exercising their "right to speak and to vote."

Still, the difficulty of overcoming the Rodriguez precedent has led many education advocates to forgo federal courts in favor of state courts.

Nearly every state constitution guarantees the right to an adequate education. But "there is broad skepticism, even on the part of many legal liberals, that the Constitution of the United States gets involved in these sorts of matters," said Justin Driver, a law professor at the University of Chicago and an expert on education litigation.

Mr. Rebell, the plaintiffs' lawyer, represented New York students for 13 years in a state-level case, which led to a landmark 2003 ruling in the students' favor over equitable school funding. But he said he continued to believe in the importance of a federal strategy. He said the civics case would make a novel, and nonpartisan, appeal to the nation's most prominent judges and justices.

"Schools are the place where students can, and should, learn about democratic institutions, their importance, their values and disposition," Mr. Rebell said. "I'm banking on the fact that what you might call establishment Republicans like John Roberts will really look at this on the merits, and will consider the broad implications."

Chief Justice Roberts recently rebuked Mr. Trump for referring to a judge who ruled against the administration's asylum policy as an "Obama judge" — and in doing so, offered a civics lesson of sorts on the independence of the judiciary.

History and civics have become curricular "stepchildren," said Luther Spoehr, a professor of history and education at Brown University in Providence, because of the pressure on schools to raise test scores in reading and math and prepare children for work in an unforgiving economy.

Though he acknowledged that standardized tests are unpopular with many parents and teachers, Professor Spoehr said that without higher-stakes exams in government or history, schools would probably never give priority to those subjects.

"What's taught is what's tested," he said.

Even if the Rhode Island lawsuit is not legally successful, he said he hoped it would create political pressure for better education in citizenship.

Aleita Cook, the plaintiff, is finally getting a powerful civics lesson by participating in the case. Though she will soon graduate from the Providence Career & Technical Academy, with plans to study photography in college, she said she wanted Rhode Island public schools to improve for her siblings' sake.

"I don't know what I'm supposed to know," she said. "We're hoping we win this lawsuit and change it to where my younger brothers can have a really good education, and go into adulthood knowing how to vote, how to do taxes, and learning basic things that you should know going into the real world."

In Novel Tactic on Climate Change, Citizens Sue Their Governments

BY JOHN SCHWARTZ | MAY 10, 2016

GLOBAL WARMING IS already disrupting the planet's weather. Now it is having an impact on the courts as well, as adults and children around the world try to enlist the judiciary in their efforts to blunt climate change.

In the United States, an environmental law nonprofit is suing the federal government on behalf of 21 young plaintiffs. Individuals in Pakistan and New Zealand have sued to force their governments to take stronger action to fight climate change. A farmer in Peru has sued a giant German energy utility over its part in causing global warming.

And while the arguments can be unconventional and surprising, some of the suits are making progress.

Last month, a federal magistrate judge in Oregon startled many legal experts by allowing the lawsuit filed on behalf of 21 teenagers and children to go forward, despite motions from the Obama administration and fossil fuel companies to dismiss it; the suit would force the government to take more aggressive action against climate change. The ruling by the magistrate judge, Thomas M. Coffin, now goes to Federal District Court to be accepted or rejected.

Michael B. Gerrard, the director of the Sabin Center for Climate Change Law at Columbia Law School, called the ruling a potential landmark.

"It is the first time a federal court has suggested that government may have a constitutional duty to combat climate change, and that individuals can sue to enforce that right," he said.

Other legal scholars were skeptical that the case would progress much further.

"The constitutional claims are novel, to say the least," said David M. Uhlmann, a former federal prosecutor of environmental crimes who teaches law at the University of Michigan. "I have a hard time

Victoria Barrett, 17, is a New York high school student and a plaintiff in a climate change lawsuit brought by Our Children's Trust.

seeing the case succeeding in the Supreme Court, if it gets that far, and it may not even survive review in the Ninth Circuit."

The young plaintiffs, led by the environmental law nonprofit Our Children's Trust, argued that the Obama administration and the administrations before it had ample evidence of the risks of climate change and "willfully ignored this impending harm."

Victoria Barrett, one of the plaintiffs, from Westchester County, N.Y., said that older generations had ignored the threat to the planet even as the scientific evidence of warming became undeniable.

The current plans and efforts to battle climate change are not enough, Ms. Barrett, 17, said, adding that her generation, with its passion and social media tools, would make a difference.

"We want our children to look back in the textbooks and say, 'Oh, our parents' generation — they really fought for us,' " she said.

The lawsuit calls for the courts to order the government to stop the "permitting, authorizing and subsidizing of fossil fuels" — by, for example, canceling plans for projects like a liquefied natural gas export terminal in Oregon — and "to develop a national plan to restore Earth's energy balance, and implement that national plan so as to stabilize the climate system."

Julia Olson, the executive director and chief legal counsel for Our Children's Trust, helped form the organization in 2010 in collaboration with the iMatter Youth Movement, then known as Kids vs. Global Warming.

In an interview, Ms. Olson said the goal was to pursue action against climate change in the courts as a human rights issue, and in the name of young people. "Most of them can't vote," she said, "and they don't have the money to lobby."

Youth-oriented climate groups put out calls for volunteers, and Ms. Olson found herself with more than enough enthusiastic young activists willing to be plaintiffs. The organization is financed in part by individual contributions and institutional funding from groups like the Rockefeller Brothers Fund, which contributes heavily to environmental causes.

An earlier federal suit from Our Children's Trust failed in 2012; the organization is also pursuing several lawsuits at the state level and collaborating on a number of international suits.

It scored a victory in Washington State recently, when Judge Hollis R. Hill of King County Superior Court ordered the State Department of Ecology to develop an emissions reduction rule in response to a legal challenge from Our Children's Trust.

As for the federal case, Ms. Olson said, "We are optimistic that the decision will affirm the findings and the recommendations and put us on a track to a trial."

The Our Children's Trust suit is part of a wave of citizen actions to take on climate change.

In Pakistan, Ashgar Leghari, a law student, sued the government last year over delays in carrying out a national climate change policy that could help reduce the heavy floods and droughts that threaten the country's food and energy security, as well as the Leghari family's farm.

A court ordered the Pakistani government in September to form a climate change commission to address what Justice Syed Mansoor Ali Shah said "appears to be the most serious threat facing Pakistan."

In November, the farmer in Peru, Saul Luciano Lliuya, sued the German utility RWE for its proportional contribution to global climate change. The effects of increasingly extreme weather such as drought can make farming a more precarious proposition, but Mr. Luciano's fears are focused on Palcacocha Lake, which sits above his town and farm and is being filled to overflowing, he said, by meltwater from nearby glaciers.

"We could see the glaciers melting," he said. "They were disappearing year by year. Somebody has to be made responsible."

An engineer he knew put him in touch with the environmental group Germanwatch, which found him a German lawyer. While it might seem bizarre for a farmer in Peru to sue a utility in Germany, Noah Walker-Crawford, an adviser to the group, said Germany's laws seemed auspicious for such a suit.

"It would be quite difficult to sue in the U.S. or Saudi Arabia," he said.

The German courts have accepted the case, but a representative of the company, Klaus-Peter Kress, said, "RWE does not see a legal basis for this type of claim."

In New Zealand, a law student, Sarah Lorraine Thomson, said she had been inspired to take legal action by the Our Children's Trust suit and a 2015 decision by a court in the Netherlands that ordered the Dutch government to take more forceful action to reduce greenhouse gas emissions.

"Hearing about those cases was a kick in the butt — they were just ordinary people, too — I felt that I really had no excuse," Ms. Thomson wrote in an email.

Xiuhtezcatl Martinez at home in Boulder, Colo., last month. He is a plaintiff in an Oregon case against the federal government over climate change.

Her lawsuit against the New Zealand government has been filed, but no hearing date has been set.

Ms. Olson of Our Children's Trust said that the cases in the United States and abroad "build on one another."

Xiuhtezcatl Martinez, a 16-year-old high school student and hip-hop artist from Boulder, Colo., who became a plaintiff in the Oregon case after getting involved in one of the state lawsuits sponsored by Our Children's Trust, said that because "climate change is really the defining issue of our time, there is no lawsuit of greater importance happening anywhere in the country."

If this suit fails, he said, he expects new ones will be filed. "The evidence will only get stronger," he added.

Some of the arguments in the Oregon lawsuit surprised legal experts, and cases that extend rights in innovative ways tend to be long shots. A lawsuit brought against fossil fuel companies and utilities by the citizens of Kivalina, Alaska, a coastal town battered by climate forces, was dismissed by the United States Court of Appeals for the Ninth Circuit in 2009.

But courts do blaze new paths, establishing rights to, for example, same-sex marriage.

"Most novel arguments crash and burn, but some soar," Professor Gerrard said. "It's often hard to predict in advance which is which."

Meet the Teenagers Leading a Climate Change Movement

BY ALEXANDRA YOON-HENDRICKS | JULY 21, 2018

WASHINGTON — Some of them met on Instagram. Others coordinated during lunchtime phone conferences. Most of them haven't even graduated from high school.

The teenagers behind Zero Hour — an environmentally focused, creatively minded and technologically savvy nationwide coalition — are trying to build a youth-led movement to sound the alarm and call for action on climate change and environmental justice.

For the last year, a tight-knit group spanning both coasts has been organizing on social media. The teenagers kicked off their campaign with a protest on Saturday at the National Mall in Washington, along with sister marches across the country.

As sea levels rise, ice caps melt and erratic weather affects communities across the globe, they say time is running out to address climate change. The core organizing group of about 20 met with almost 40 federal lawmakers about their platforms on Thursday, and hope to inspire other teenagers to step up and demand change.

"The march is a launch. It isn't, 'That's it, we're done,'" said Jamie Margolin, the founder of Zero Hour. "It means it doesn't give them an excuse to be like, 'I don't know what the kids want.' It's like, 'Yes, you do.'"

They are trying to prove the adults wrong, to show that people their age are taking heed of what they see as the greatest crisis threatening their generation.

"In our generation when we talk about climate change, they're like: 'Ha ha, that's so funny. It's not something we'll have to deal with,'" said Nadia Nazar, Zero Hour's art director. "'Oh, yeah, the polar bears will just die, the seas will just rise.' They don't understand the actual caliber of the destruction."

The group is building off the momentum of other recent youth-led movements, such as the nationwide March for Our Lives rallies against gun violence.

"No one gives you an organizing guide of how to raise thousands of dollars, how to get people on board, how to mobilize," Ms. Margolin said. "There was no help. It was just me floundering around with Dory-like determination, like, 'Just keep swimming,' " she said, referring to the Disney movie "Finding Nemo."

At the Sierra Club's Washington headquarters on Wednesday, as Zero Hour members continued to make preparations, six of the coalition's leaders and founding members discussed how they became involved with the group, and why they think it's one of young people's best shots at creating a healthy, sustainable environment.

'WE ARE ON THE VERGE OF SOMETHING AMAZING'
Jamie Margolin, 16, Seattle

"I've always planned my future in ifs," Ms. Margolin said. If climate change hasn't destroyed this, if the environment hasn't become that.

So for the last few years, Ms. Margolin has worked to raise awareness about climate justice issues. A passionate writer, she went through an "op-ed phase," submitting essays to publications, like one titled "An Open Letter to Climate Change Deniers" published in the monthly magazine Teen Ink.

Still, Ms. Margolin thought that she and other young people could — and should — be doing more.

"I had had this idea building up since January, since the Women's March" last year, Ms. Margolin said. "The kind of idea that was nagging me and you try to ignore, but it's an idea poking you."

At a Princeton University summer program last year, she met other teenagers interested in taking action on climate change and created Zero Hour. They began to plan a huge protest in the nation's capital. On social media, Ms. Margolin espoused factoids and reached out to other young activists.

"The march is a launch," Jamie Margolin, the founder of Zero Hour, said of Saturday's demonstration in Washington. "It isn't, 'That's it, we're done.'"

A professed climate justice advocate, Ms. Margolin has kept the movement inclusive, putting the stories and concerns of those most directly affected by environmental issues at the heart of Zero Hour's mission. Youths from in and around the Standing Rock Sioux Reservation spoke on Saturday, and others repeatedly called attention to those killed during Hurricane Maria and threatened by rising sea levels in the Marshall Islands.

Since starting Zero Hour, Ms. Margolin said she had been overwhelmed by the response from people of all ages. Dozens of environmental advocacy groups and nonprofits have approached the coalition, looking to donate to or sponsor it.

"We flipped the scenario as the underdog. We've proven ourselves," she said. "We are on the verge of something amazing. We're going to change history."

Kallan Benson has encouraged other young people to express their concerns about the climate through art.

SHOWING A MOVEMENT'S ARTISTIC SIDE
Kallan Benson, 14, Crownsville, Md.

When Ms. Benson was planning a trip to the Peoples Climate March last year with her family, she knew she wanted to make a statement.

Ms. Benson doesn't consider herself an artist. But a 24-foot-wide play parachute that she covered in a gigantic monarch butterfly design and hundreds of signatures from children in her community became a canvas for her to display the dire future she and coming generations may face, and express optimism that they will overcome it.

A chance encounter with the son of the founder of the nonprofit Mother Earth Project led Ms. Benson to encourage children around the world to create parachutes of their own made of recycled bedsheets (to be "environmentally conscious," of course).

Inspired by the AIDS Memorial Quilt that has been unfurled on the National Mall in years past, some of those parachutes, sent from every continent except Antarctica, were laid out on the grass during Saturday's march.

"The original idea was, 'We got to get them on the National Mall,' but then we thought that, 'Well that shouldn't be our first exhibit; it's a little ambitious,' " Ms. Benson said.

"Then we talked to Zero Hour and they were like, 'Hey, why don't you bring them out?' " she continued. "I never imagined it would get this far."

WHERE BUSINESS AND THE ENVIRONMENT MEET
Madelaine Tew, 15, Teaneck, N.J.

As Zero Hour's director of finance, Ms. Tew has had to get creative about securing funds and grants.

On the day of a deadline for a major grant — $16,000 from the Common Sense Fund — Ms. Tew's school was hosting an event where

Madelaine Tew's finance team has raised about $70,000 for Zero Hour.

seniors gave presentations about their internships. But she knew the grant would be a huge boost for Zero Hour.

"So I went to the nurse and was like: 'Oh, I have cramps. Can I lie down with my computer?' " she said. "Then I just went in and wrote the whole grant."

Her stunt paid off. Zero Hour secured the grant, and now Ms. Tew's finance team, made up of students just like her, has raised about $70,000 for the coalition.

Ms. Tew, who attends a magnet high school where she takes classes in business and finance, has been involved in clubs to get the school and local businesses to adopt more renewable practices. But before meeting Ms. Margolin at the Princeton summer program last year, she thought those local efforts were "as far as you can go" for someone her age.

"It shifted from youth being a limitation to 'it doesn't matter,' " Ms. Tew said.

Though the practices of big corporations can sometimes anger environmentalists, for Ms. Tew, combining "my love for business and my care, my concern for climate" just makes sense.

"In many cases you can see how the environmental movement can be rooted in the way we do business," she said.

That could take the form of encouraging companies to divest from fossil fuel industries or having local communities build their own solar or wind grids.

"We're not just talking about building more cooperative farms," Ms. Tew said, but also figuring out how to integrate ethical and sustainable environmental policies into business so "we can continue the American economy's future."

'REPPING THE YOUNGER GENERATION'
Iris Fen Gillingham, 18, Livingston Manor, N.Y.

When three floods in the mid- to late 2000s swept through the vegetable farm Iris Fen Gillingham's family owned in the Catskill

Iris Fen Gillingham believes that sustainable lifestyles are essential for the success of her generation.

Mountains, the topsoil was washed away and their equipment was submerged, eliminating their main source of income.

The floods devastated Ms. Gillingham's family, which has always lived "very consciously with the land and with nature," she said. Even her name, Iris Fen, like the flower and marshy wetland behind her house, alludes to that attachment.

"I have a pair of mittens that are made out of one of our Icelandic sheep, Rosalie," Ms. Gillingham said. "My brother named her, I remember her being born and I've seen her grow up and my mom sheering her and spinning the wool."

So when landsmen came to explore the possibility of hydraulic fracturing — a technique of oil and gas extraction also known as fracking — in their neighborhood when she was about 10, Ms. Gillingham joined her father, an environmental activist, in speaking out at local meetings, often as the youngest in the room.

"It was always myself repping the younger generation," Ms. Gillingham said. "Part of that was my brother and I saying, 'We don't want to play on contaminated soil,' " (The Environmental Protection Agency has concluded that fracking can contaminate drinking water in some circumstances.)

But part of it was also knowing firsthand how essential a sustainable lifestyle — growing food at home, conscious spending, building greener homes — will be for her generation.

"We're setting aside our differences and we are building a family and a community using our skills and our creativity," Ms. Gillingham said of the movement. "We're having fun, we're laughing with each other, but we're also talking about some pretty serious issues and injustices happening in this country."

LINKING ANIMAL RIGHTS AND ENVIRONMENTALISM
Nadia Nazar, 16, Baltimore

Before joining Zero Hour, Nadia Nazar considered herself mostly an animal-rights activist. When she was 12, she saw a PETA video on slaughterhouses and immediately became a vegetarian.

"I had just gotten a cat," Ms. Nazar said. "What if my cat was that cow?"

She got her start as an activist by trying to persuade people in her neighborhood not to go to SeaWorld, which has been criticized over its treatment of animals. ("I was slightly successful in that.")

Then she dug deeper into the root causes of animal suffering and death.

"I found out how so many species are endangered by climate change, and how many are dying and going towards extinction that we caused ourselves," Ms. Nazar said.

During a class, she stumbled upon Ms. Margolin's Teen Ink essay and followed her on Instagram. And a little over a year ago, when Ms. Nazar saw a post by Ms. Margolin calling for action, she knew it was her chance to put her artistic skills to use. As art director, she helped

Nadia Nazar got her start as an activist by trying to persuade people not to go to SeaWorld.

organize a smaller art festival on Friday, and created the majority of the graphic elements for the coalition.

"Her story said: 'I'm going to do it. Who wants to join me?'" Ms. Nazar said. She immediately messaged Ms. Margolin. She was in.

WORKING TOGETHER TOWARD A BIGGER GOAL
Zanagee Artis, 18, Clinton, Conn.

Zanagee Artis's journey as an environmentalist began in the same place many other budding activists get their start — in a high school club.

During his junior year, he had big ambitions for his school: the building facilities department would finally start recycling white paper, students would start composting their food waste and the lunchroom would be free of plastic foam trays.

"I'm going to accomplish all these things and I'm going to go to the administration and tell them, 'Stuff needs to change,' " Mr. Artis said.

Zanagee Artis said he was inspired by Ms. Margolin's enthusiasm to do "a big, big thing."

But, he said, "nothing ever happened." Mr. Artis said the problem was clear: Without engaging other students who might be interested, change was unlikely to happen.

So he started a sustainability committee within the school's National Honor Society, and the results spoke for themselves. The group was able to buy the school an aquaponic system — a tank-based farming system that combines hydroponics (water-based planting) and aquaculture (fish cultivation) — and raise $700 to install water bottle refilling stations.

"So we accomplished all these things because we worked together as a community, and that's how I feel about the climate movement," he said.

Still, Mr. Artis said he "really didn't think I could do much" beyond his local community until he met Ms. Margolin and Ms. Tew last summer at Princeton. Inspired by Ms. Margolin's enthusiasm to do "a big,

big thing," Mr. Artis became Zero Hour's logistics director, in charge of submitting permits for Saturday's march, estimating attendance numbers, checking for counterprotests and helping sister marches with logistical issues.

"I was like, 'Yes!' " he said with a satisfying clap. " 'Let's do it.' "

Young People Are Suing the Trump Administration Over Climate Change. She's Their Lawyer.

BY JOHN SCHWARTZ | OCT. 23, 2018

EUGENE, ORE. — Julia Olson climbed the slope of Spencer Butte, taking the steeper of the two paths. Near the summit, shrouding pines suddenly gave way to a vista of the Cascades. On this day, summer wildfires, their season lengthened by climate change, put a haze in the sky.

The climb and return, which she can power through in an hour, is a head-clearing ritual for Ms. Olson, an environmental attorney. It is also a place to compose the soaring language of opening and closing arguments. "I do my legal thinking here," she said.

If all goes as planned, Ms. Olson will deliver her opening argument on Monday in a landmark federal lawsuit against the Trump administration on behalf of 21 plaintiffs, ages 11 to 22, who are demanding that the government fight climate change. It is a case that could test whether the judicial branch has a major role to play in dealing with global warming, and whether there is a constitutional right to a stable and safe climate.

The young plaintiffs claim that the government's actions, and inaction, in the face of global warming violate their "fundamental constitutional rights to freedom from deprivation of life, liberty, and property." Their age is central to their argument: For older Americans, the potentially catastrophic effects of climate change are a problem, but ultimately an abstract one. Today's children, however, will be dealing with disaster within their lifetimes; the youngest of the plaintiffs, Levi Draheim, will be just 33 in 2040, the year by which a United Nations scientific panel now expects some of the biggest crises to begin.

But as of now, less than a week before the trial is scheduled to start in Federal District Court in Eugene, whether the young people will get

Julia Olson on a hike near Eugene, Ore. She is representing 21 young people who are suing the federal government.

their day in court is still an open question. On Friday, Chief Justice John G. Roberts Jr. granted a Trump administration request to put a brief hold on the proceedings to consider government filings that could derail the case.

It is unclear how long the delay will last, or what the outcome will be. The Supreme Court could even dismiss the litigation, though that would be unusual at this early stage.

The lawsuit, Juliana v. United States, is the most visible case for Ms. Olson and her nonprofit organization, Our Children's Trust. The group is involved in similar legal actions in almost every state, and other climate suits around the world.

Ms. Olson originally filed the federal suit in 2015 against the Obama administration, demanding faster action from a president already seen as friendly to environmental interests. Working under a legal principle known as the public trust doctrine, which can be used to compel the government to preserve natural resources for public use, the initial complaint stated that government officials had "willfully ignored" the dangers of burning fossil fuels.

Then came President Trump, whose administration is reversing Obama-era climate policies and encouraging the use of fossil fuels, which greatly contribute to warming. "In the view of the plaintiffs, Obama was moving too slowly, and now Trump is moving backward," said Michael B. Gerrard, director of the Sabin Center for Climate Change Law at Columbia Law School.

The young plaintiffs have demanded, among other things, that the courts force the government to "implement an enforceable national remedial plan to phase out fossil fuel emissions" in an effort to "stabilize the climate system." The courts could then supervise the government's efforts.

The Trump administration's lawyers are not arguing that climate change is a hoax. Instead, they are making similar arguments to those that the Obama administration made when it, too, tried to dismiss the case: that the young people don't have standing to sue (a legal formula requiring plaintiffs to show that, among other things, they have suffered a concrete, particular injury because of the actions of the defendant) and that the courts are the wrong place to deal with the issue.

"This lawsuit is an unconstitutional attempt to use a single Oregon court to control the entire nation's energy and climate policy," Jeffrey H. Wood, the Justice Department attorney in charge of the division representing the government, said in a statement.

But Judge Ann Aiken, who is scheduled to preside over the trial on Monday, has been receptive to the plaintiffs' theory of the case. "I have no doubt that the right to a climate system capable of sustaining human life is fundamental to a free and ordered society," she said in a November 2016 decision allowing the case to go forward.

Since then, the case has rumbled toward trial. In an earlier order in July, the Supreme Court denied a government request to intervene, but wrote that the breadth of the plaintiffs' claims was "striking," which could be taken as a note of skepticism about the case's prospects should it reach the justices.

Trial preparation has been intense at Ms. Olson's little law firm. Like many law offices, there is a conference room with a long table and computers humming, but there is also chilled kombucha on tap in the kitchen. "I've sort of addicted everybody to it," Ms. Olson said.

Before her sprint up the butte on the day I visited, Ms. Olson had already attended a morning hearing at Eugene's federal courthouse. Back at the converted 1920s bungalow that houses Our Children's Trust, she talked with some young plaintiffs who had stayed over from a campground retreat she had held the week before. The subject: what would be expected of them in their depositions.

Philip L. Gregory, another lawyer in the case, described the deposition setup, jumping up and taking positions where the young people would be seated, where their attorney would be, where the questioning attorney would be and where the videographer would be. At that point, he mimicked someone hand-cranking a camera, which got confused giggles from the smartphone generation.

"The most important rule about the deposition is to tell the truth," Mr. Gregory said. "A deposition is not a test of understanding the law of thermodynamics. It's not a test on the history of World War II."

"Or climate change," Ms. Olson interjected.

"Or climate change," he agreed.

Ms. Olson grew up in Colorado Springs. She attended the University of Colorado, Boulder, and stayed in the state to live the life of a ski bum while deciding her next move.

She took the LSAT but left the test thinking she had done poorly. "I didn't even apply to any law schools," she said. The test results were a pleasant surprise. She received her degree from Hastings College of the Law in San Francisco.

In 2010, she encountered the legal theory that would launch the climate lawsuits when she met Mary Christina Wood, a law professor at the University of Oregon.

Professor Wood had been proposing for some time that lawsuits to stop climate change could be built around the public trust doctrine. But she was no litigator, she said. Ms. Olson was.

Since then, Ms. Olson has pursued the federal case with meticulous preparation and a relentless work ethic, Professor Wood said. "This could have fizzled with anyone but Julia," she said. "She has built not just a case, but a movement."

Legal experts view Ms. Olson's chances with a measure of ambivalence.

"The claims are compelling, and the legal theory is creative," said David M. Uhlmann, a law professor at the University of Michigan and a former top Justice Department official on environmental crimes. However, he said, "It is hard to see the Supreme Court upholding a favorable verdict, if the case gets that far."

Erwin Chemerinsky, dean of the University of California, Berkeley, School of Law, pronounced himself a fan of the suit. Though he acknowledged that the courts tend to frown on creative legal theories, he noted that they do sometimes make new law in cases like Obergefell v. Hodges, which found a right to same-sex marriage, and Brown v. Board of Education, the landmark school desegregation case. "Creative lawyering there triumphed," he said. With this case, he said, "We'll see how it goes in the courts."

The plaintiffs say they are ready, having waited three years of their young lives to see the case reach a courtroom. Ms. Olson found many of them through their own environmental activism. She interviewed each of them, exploring the personal threats they faced from climate change (Levi Draheim, for example, lives on a Florida barrier island imperiled by sea-level rise).

Kelsey Juliana, the plaintiff whose name appears first in the case, is the oldest of the group at 22. Ms. Olson, she said, is "an idol of mine" who balances her legal practice with activism and motherhood.

Ms. Juliana recalled a news conference at the courthouse two days after the 2016 election, after Judge Aiken had denied a government request to dismiss the case. Despite that victory, "I was really heart-broken" about the election results, she said.

Ms. Olson came up to her and looked her in the eye. No words passed between them, but Ms. Olson's expression, she said, was eloquent. "She was basically saying, 'I see you're emotional, and that's O.K. But we still have work to do. And we're going to do it.' "

As she told the story of their silent moment, her eyes filled with tears. "It was vulnerability on both of our parts, and it was O.K. to be vulnerable," she said. "But we were also strong."

JOHN SCHWARTZ is part of the climate team. Since joining The Times in 2000, he has covered science, law, technology, the space program and more, and has written for almost every section.

CHAPTER 2

Parkland and the New Wave of Gun Control Activism

On Feb. 14, 2018, a gunman opened fire in a high school in Parkland, Fla., killing 17 people. It was hardly the first school shooting the nation had seen; for students, it was the last straw. The events that unfolded in Parkland sparked a new wave of teenage activism, as students turned their efforts toward rallying for stricter gun laws.

Emma González Leads a Student Outcry on Guns: 'This Is the Way I Have to Grieve'

BY JULIE TURKEWITZ, MATT STEVENS AND JASON M. BAILEY | FEB. 18, 2018

Students used Twitter, the news media and a courthouse rally to pressure lawmakers for gun control after a deadly shooting at a Florida high school.

FORT LAUDERDALE, FLA. — They shouted into a microphone until their voices became hoarse. They waved handmade signs. They chanted.

And sometimes, in the middle of it all, they choked up.

At the federal courthouse here on Saturday, students — including many of the very people who had to endure the trauma of a shooting on campus — continued to speak out about guns. Since Wednesday, when a gunman killed 14 students and three staff members at

Ellie Branson, center, was among the many teenage participants in the Not One More rally for gun legislation held at the federal courthouse in Fort Lauderdale, Fla., on Saturday.

Marjory Stoneman Douglas High School in Parkland, Fla., their youthful voices have resonated where those of longtime politicians have largely fallen flat.

And on Saturday, another young woman's words captivated the nation.

Speaking publicly at the rally, Emma González, a senior, pledged that her school would be the site of the nation's last mass shooting. How could she know? Because, she said, she and her peers would take it upon themselves to "change the law."

"The people in the government who are voted into power are lying to us," she said. "And us kids seem to be the only ones who notice and are prepared to call B.S."

"They say that tougher gun laws do not decrease gun violence — we call B.S.!" she continued as a chorus of supporters echoed her. "They say a good guy with a gun stops a bad guy with a gun — we call B.S.! They say guns are just tools like knives and are as dangerous as cars — we call B.S.! They say that no laws could have been able to prevent the hundreds of senseless tragedies that have occurred — we call B.S.! That us kids don't know what we're talking about, that we're too young to understand how the government works — we call B.S.!"

She wiped her eyes aggressively. Then, she urged the people in the crowd to register to vote — and to give their elected officials "a piece of your mind."

Just hours later, one video of the speech had been viewed more than 100,000 times.

In a telephone interview early Sunday, Ms. González, 18, said she was surprised by the enthusiastic reaction to her speech.

"I just got off the phone with Demi Lovato," she said. "That's not normally something that ever should have happened."

Ms. González said she was encouraged to speak out, in part, by other supportive people in her community, especially those who she said do not yet feel comfortable talking publicly.

"This is my whole world now," she said. "I cannot allow myself to stop talking about this."

A person Ms. González met at a party was killed in the shooting, she said; another person she has known for "an incredibly long time" is still in the hospital.

"Everybody needs to understand how we feel and what we went through, because if they don't, they're not going to be able to understand why we're fighting for what we're fighting for," Ms. González said.

She noted that some have criticized students for raising their voices, suggesting that they take the time to grieve instead.

"This is the way I have to grieve," Ms. González said. "I have to make sure that everybody knows that this isn't something that is allowed to happen."

Here are the voices of some other students who, like Ms. González, have spoken out in recent days.

DAVID HOGG, 17:
'WE'RE CHILDREN. YOU GUYS ARE THE ADULTS'

While David Hogg, 17, and dozens of his Stoneman Douglas classmates were hiding in the dark in the school chef's office, he interviewed them on camera about their views on gun policy. Mr. Hogg, a senior and the student news director, later told The New York Times that lawmakers must make schools safer.

"We need to do something," he said. "We need to get out there and be politically active. Congress needs to get over their political bias with each other and work toward saving children's lives."

Referring to politicians, Mr. Hogg told CNN: "We're children. You guys are the adults."

CARLY NOVELL, 17: 'THIS IS ABOUT GUNS'

Hours after the mass shooting, surviving students turned to social media to discuss gun control. They addressed the prevalence of such attacks and why someone with a mental illness can buy a gun.

"Guns give these disgusting people the ability to kill other human beings," Carly Novell, a 17-year-old senior who is an editor for the school's quarterly magazine, wrote on Twitter. "This IS about guns."

In a video interview with The Times, Ms. Novell said she was trying to use her anger fruitfully.

"People always talk about gun control and how things need to change, but nothing ever does," she said. "And that is so frustrating."

TYRA HEMANS, 19: 'I WANT TO TALK WITH' TRUMP

The public outcry from some Stoneman Douglas students was vastly different from the response of survivors of the Columbine High School shooting in 1999. Those students two decades ago did not turn to activism as they grieved.

In contrast, Tyra Hemans, a senior at Stoneman Douglas, brought a poster featuring the word "ENOUGH" to a funeral for one of her

Ellie Branson at the Not One More rally to support gun legislation held at the federal courthouse in Fort Lauderdale, Fla.

classmates on Friday. She said she also wanted to deliver a message to President Trump.

"I want our politicians to stop thinking about money and start thinking about all these lives we had lost," she said. "I want to talk with him about changing these laws."

DANIELA PALACIOS, 16: 'CHANGE IS GOING TO COME OF THIS'

Among those who attended Saturday's rally was Daniela Palacios, 16, a sophomore at another Broward County high school, Cypress Bay.

This was her first protest, she said, and she stood with her mother, a tiny gold cross on a chain around her neck.

Returning to school after the shooting at Stoneman Douglas had been difficult, she explained, and she said she was there to call for a ban on firearms like the semiautomatic AR-15 rifle used by the gunman.

"Wherever you bump into someone, there is the fear that they're the next shooter," she said, "and every bell is a gunshot."

"I feel like some change is going to come of this," she went on, her voice barely audible amid the roar of the crowd. "I feel hopeful."

ELLIE BRANSON, 16:
'CAN YOU INCLUDE THE NAMES OF THE VICTIMS?'

When the protest ended, a group of teenagers stayed behind, chanting and hugging — and chanting again.

"It could have been us," one sign read. "My friend died for what?" said another.

"No more guns! No more guns! No more guns!" they yelled.

Among those leading the group was Ellie Branson, 16, a junior from South Broward High School. She wore a yellow and white T-shirt, her cheeks wet with tears.

When the protest finally ended, she texted a reporter.

"Can you include the names of the victims?" she asked. "Their names are more important than mine."

JULIE TURKEWITZ reported from Fort Lauderdale, Fla., and MATT STEVENS and JASON M. BAILEY from New York. JACK BEGG contributed research.

Highlights: Students Call for Action Across Nation; Florida Lawmakers Fail to Take Up Assault Rifle Bill

BY JULIE TURKEWITZ AND ANEMONA HARTOCOLLIS | FEB. 20, 2018

CORAL SPRINGS, FLA. — Driven by rage and grief over one of the deadliest school shootings in modern American history, students from across the country were taking action in hopes of pushing their lawmakers to rethink their positions on gun control, even as the Florida State House rejected a move on Tuesday to consider a bill that would ban assault rifles.

From California to Florida, teenagers walked out of classes, stopped traffic and made stirring speeches calling out their elders for inaction.

Students from Marjory Stoneman Douglas High School in Parkland, Fla., where 17 people were killed last week, traveled on Tuesday to Tallahassee, the state capital, to call for an assault weapons ban. The direct appeal to the Legislature follows protests outside schools, social media appeals and national television appearances.

• Assault rifles have become a particular target of the latest gun-control campaign. The police say the suspect in last week's massacre, Nikolas Cruz, was able to kill 17 people in just six minutes by wielding a semiautomatic weapon, an AR-15 rifle.

• President Trump on Tuesday ordered the Justice Department to propose regulations to ban so-called bump stocks, which can convert a semiautomatic gun into an automatic weapon like the one used last year in the Las Vegas shooting.

• A Washington Post/ABC News opinion poll released on Tuesday showed that 77 percent of Americans believe the Republican-controlled Congress is not doing enough to prevent mass shootings, with 62 percent saying President Trump has not done enough. On

Monday, the White House indicated that Mr. Trump was open to supporting a bipartisan effort to revise federal background checks for prospective gun buyers.

• The actor George Clooney and his wife, Amal, said Tuesday that they would donate $500,000 to a nationwide protest against gun violence planned for next month by the Stoneman Douglas High students. The announcement inspired similar gifts from other big-name Hollywood figures, including the producer Jeffrey Katzenberg and his wife, Marilyn, Oprah Winfrey, and Steven Spielberg and his wife, Kate Capshaw.

• As of Monday, two survivors of the shooting remained hospitalized in fair condition at Broward Health North, and two others remained in fair condition at Broward Health Medical Center in Fort Lauderdale.

• The Florida shooting has renewed attention on state laws that allow a judge to take away weapons from people who are deemed dangerous, known as "red flag" laws. Some governors have shown a willingness to change their mind on gun restrictions, but other simply dug in on their stances.

• In Florida, an AR-15 is easier to buy than a handgun. The AR-15 has become one of the weapons of choice for mass killers, and research has tried to explain the high rate of mass shootings in the United States.

THE FLORIDA HOUSE REJECTS A MOTION TO TAKE UP A BILL BANNING ASSAULT RIFLES.
State Representative Kionne McGhee, a Democrat from Miami, asked for an unusual procedural move to consider his legislation, which had been filed earlier in the session but was never scheduled for a hearing.

"The shooting in Parkland demands extraordinary action," Mr. McGhee said Tuesday on the House floor, as a different group of Stoneman Douglas High students, who had previously arrived, peered down from the gallery.

Students from Stoneman Douglas High, as they prepared in Coral Springs, Fla., to leave for Tallahassee on Tuesday.

The motion failed, 36 to 71, in a vote along party lines. At least one student burst into tears, Mr. McGhee said. One girl covered her mouth in despair, as a woman patted her arm to comfort her. The episode lasted 2 minutes and 38 seconds.

As the news began to spread aboard a bus of students headed to the capital, Anthony Lopez, 16, a junior, slammed his head back on the bus seat. He placed a hand on his forehead. "That's infuriating," he said. "They're acting inhuman."

"The one fear we have is that nothing will change," he added.

A similar proposal filed last year in the wake of the Pulse nightclub shooting in Orlando also went nowhere.

Republican leaders in the Legislature have said they would consider more modest proposals, including raising the minimum age to buy assault rifles, before the session ends in March. The Miami Herald reported that legislators in both the Florida House and Senate were also drafting legislation to limit access to semiautomatic rifles, after years of reluctance. That plan would bar people under 21 from possession of an assault rifle, and would require buyers to wait three days before purchasing any kind of rifle.

"The House looks forward to working with the Governor and Senate to find solutions to fulfill government's primary mission — to keep its citizens — its children safe," said Richard Corcoran, the Republican speaker of the House, in a statement. "And it is our goal to give these collective solutions the serious review and consideration they deserve."

In session later on Tuesday, the House did approve a resolution declaring pornography a public health risk. Representative Carlos Guillermo Smith, a Democrat from Orlando, questioned why the pornography proposal was given priority. Implicit in his question was why the assault weapons ban was not.

"Has anyone ever been killed as a result of the health implications of pornography?" he asked.

OUR REPORTER RODE WITH STUDENTS AS THEY TRAVELED TO TALLAHASSEE.
Buoyed by viral tweets and media interviews, several Stoneman Douglas High students who survived the attack have been vocal about wanting change since the shooting. Their message: We've been there. Listen to us.

At first, the students gained notice for their raw, emotional reactions in the immediate aftermath of the shooting. The emotion hasn't receded, but efforts to channel their grief into legislative change — like 18-year-old Emma González's appeal for gun laws — have been widely praised.

On Tuesday, teenagers from the school, gripping pillows and sleeping bags and carrying doughnuts and candy, packed a grocery store parking lot in Coral Springs, Fla., to begin the more than 400-mile journey to Tallahassee.

Their goal: convincing lawmakers to pass a slate of gun control bills in a state that has been among the friendliest to firearm owners in the nation.

Many had come straight from the funeral of one of the dead. They hugged their parents goodbye and loaded backpacks into the bellies of three buses. Dozens climbed aboard.

In a telephone interview from the bus, Sarah Chadwick, 16, a junior, said the social media response to the students had been overwhelming, but she wanted everyone to know: "We see your support, we see what you're doing."

The students felt they had the "best voices to listen to right now," along with other survivors of shootings, and that Twitter had allowed them to reach more people than they would have thought possible, she said.

"We have stuff to say, and we won't be silenced after a matter of days, or even weeks," she said.

By the seventh hour of the trip, students on the bus had become aware of Mr. Clooney's donation and the supportive remarks made by other celebrities.

But as they strategized in the back of the bus, some worried that Mr. Clooney's star power and liberal activism would swallow their voices and push conservatives away.

"The minute they don't see our faces anymore, and they just see the Hollywood elite, they're going to stop taking it seriously," said Chris Grady, 18, a senior with a mop of curly hair.

Mr. Grady said he had enlisted in the Army a few months back, but that the attack at his school had made him think hard about whether that was the path he wanted to take.

"As it stands right now, the real danger is at home, not abroad," he said. "So this is where I want to be — right at the heart of the movement."

"I wasn't sure what I wanted to study," he continued. "And now for sure I'll be getting my degree in political science."

Finally, around 10 p.m., the three buses of students from Stoneman Douglas High rolled into the parking lot of a Tallahassee high school. They had arrived.

"Oh. My. God," said one teenager, peering out the bus window. "It's so many people."

A crowd of people from Leon High had gathered in front of the red brick building to support and cheer the Stoneman Douglas group.

In the morning, the students will break into groups and meet with some 70 elected officials. Gov. Rick Scott is expected to give them two hours.

Mallory Muller, a Stoneman Douglas High student, hugged a teddy bear to her chest.

"The whole bus ride here I was very anxious," she said. "You have the nervousness about — what happens? And kind of scared for your own safety."

"We know what we're doing tomorrow is big," she went on, "so I think there is that buildup tomorrow, too. That pressure."

STUDENTS ELSEWHERE IN FLORIDA MARCH IN A SPONTANEOUS SHOW OF SUPPORT.

Before marching south toward Stoneman Douglas High, dozens of students from West Boca Raton High School first gathered in the courtyard of their school for a peaceful protest — 17 minutes of silence for the 17 victims — but then someone opened a door and walked out, and others followed, a videotape of the scene aired by WPTV showed.

"Everybody started walking," one student told the news channel. "It felt like half the school was walking."

As the students walked south on U.S. Highway 441, sheriff's deputies lined the road to direct traffic and keep them safe, but did not interfere. The distance between the two schools is about 10 miles.

The march from Boca Raton surprised Broward County officials, who said they had heard nothing about the protest. Todd DeAngelis, a spokesman for the city of Parkland, said the authorities abruptly assembled an escort by law enforcement and organized water stations on a day when the temperature was in the low 80s.

HUNDREDS OF MOURNERS, INCLUDING MILITARY, HONORED A J.R.O.T.C. MEMBER AT HIS FUNERAL.

In a rare honor, the United States Military Academy offered the member, Peter Wang, 15, the realization of a lifelong dream: admission to West Point, posthumously. The academy said it was extending the offer in recognition of his "heroic actions" during the shooting.

Mr. Wang was last seen holding a door open at Stoneman Douglas High so that others could escape, Ernie Rospierski, a teacher who survived, told CBS News.

Relatives of Mr. Wang, a cadet in the school's Junior Reserve Officers' Training Corps program, described him as modest and not interested in status, but eager to serve and help others.

At his funeral on Tuesday, the military mourners acknowledged him as one of them. They came in echoes of the uniform that he had once proudly worn: Marine and Navy dress blues, high school R.O.T.C. members in their dress uniforms, others wearing camouflage fatigues. Veterans were in attendance, as well.

"We came down to represent," said Jeff Colopy, vice commander of American Legion Post 157 in Margate, Fla., to "pay tribute to one of our fallen comrades. In our eyes, he was military."

Lying in an open coffin in the small chapel at Kraeer Funeral Home and Cremation Center in Coral Springs, with a military honor guard at either end, Mr. Wang wore his uniform. A line of mourners stretched out of the chapel, with scores more waiting under a tent outside.

Mr. Wang was one of three Junior R.O.T.C. cadets who were killed in the shooting; the others were Martin Duque, 14, and Alaina Petty, also 14.

The shooting suspect, Mr. Cruz, had also been a member of his school's Army Junior R.O.T.C., and had "excelled" in air rifle marksmanship contests with other schools in the area in a program that was supported by a grant from the National Rifle Association Foundation, according to The Associated Press. He was wearing his maroon Junior R.O.T.C. emblem polo shirt when he was arrested after the shooting, The A.P. reported.

"We all have those shirts," Angelyse Perez, an 18-year-old senior and a company commander, told The Washington Post. "We're never wearing them again. We're going to destroy them all."

PROTESTS RIPPLE OUT ACROSS THE NATION.

At rallies across the country on Monday and Tuesday, students made pleas for gun control and declared that while they might not be old enough to vote, they were old enough to change society.

A crowd of students stood on the steps of the squat, red brick public library in Toms River, N.J., on Monday, a school holiday, to express their solidarity with the fallen Parkland students and teachers.

In Chicago, students from the South Side, where gun violence has been a problem, began organizing to demand gun control legislation.

In Battle Creek, Mich., dozens of students walked out of Harper Creek High School on Tuesday to protest gun violence in schools.

And in Bakersfield, Calif., about a dozen students and 80 adults joined a protest on Monday. "Listening to how worried my mother was dropping me off Friday morning after the shooting was one of the worst things I've had to listen to in a while," Lucy Brown, a member of the Bakersfield High School Young Democrats Club who helped organize the protests, told bakersfield.com.

SOME STATES ARE CONSIDERING 'RED FLAG' LAWS.

The Florida shooting has renewed attention on state laws that allow a judge to remove weapons from people deemed dangerous, known as "red flag" laws. The measures are frequently supported by Democrats, but opposed by many Republicans and gun rights advocates.

State Representative Arthur O'Neill, a Republican from Connecticut, one of only five states to have such laws, has said he would write to legislative leaders in other states to urge them to adopt similar laws. "Unfortunately, this law is not as widely known as it should be," Mr. O'Neill said last week in a statement.

In Pennsylvania, State Senator Daylin Leach on Tuesday announced that he was proposing red flag legislation.

"Frequently, when there are mass shootings, we see stories about how the shooter made threats, posted on social media, and did all kinds of things showing that he was a danger to the community, yet nothing was done," said Mr. Leach, a Democrat, in a statement. "My new bill would allow a judge to separate dangerous people from their guns until they get the help they need."

Similar bills have been proposed this year in other states, including Hawaii and Illinois. The N.R.A. has often spoken against red flag legislation, saying the judges' orders can infringe on a person's Second Amendment rights when no crime has been committed.

GOVERNORS IN VERMONT AND OHIO HAVE SIGNALED A SHIFT TOWARD TIGHTER CONTROLS.

In Vermont, a progressive but rural state with largely permissive gun laws, Gov. Phil Scott, a Republican, initially told reporters the state's gun laws did not need to be updated after the Florida shooting, according to news reports. But Mr. Scott changed his tone a day later, after the authorities accused an 18-year-old student of planning an attack at his school in Fair Haven, Vt.

"We must determine if we are truly doing all we can to prevent violence," Mr. Scott said, and asked legislative leaders to identify policy changes and have "an open conversation about gun safety."

In Ohio, Gov. John Kasich, a Republican who has previously touted support from the N.R.A., made an impassioned plea for Congress to consider restrictions on assault weapons.

"Would you feel as though your Second Amendment rights would be eroded because you couldn't buy a God darn AR-15?" Mr. Kasich, who voted for an assault weapons ban in 1994 while in Congress, asked on CNN. "These are the things that have to be looked at."

In Kentucky, Gov. Matt Bevin, a Republican, repeated a position he took in late January after a 15-year-old shot and killed two fellow students at a high school in Benton, Ky. Mr. Bevin suggested in an interview with The Cincinnati Enquirer that it was violent video games and culture, rather than guns, that should be restricted.

In Rhode Island, Gina Raimondo, the Democratic governor, reiterated calls for stronger state and federal measures.

"We need to outlaw military-style assault weapons like our neighbors have in Massachusetts and Connecticut," Ms. Raimondo told The Providence Journal, also calling for a ban on high-capacity magazines.

And in Idaho, according to The Statesman, Gov. C.L. Otter, a Republican, suggested there was little more the state could do to prevent school shootings. "I think we've done what we can do," he said.

JULIE TURKEWITZ reported from Coral Springs, Fla., and ANEMONA HARTOCOLIS from New York. Reporting was contributed by ALAN BLINDER from Parkland, Fla.; NEIL REISNER from Coral Springs, Fla.; DANIEL VICTOR, MATT STEVENS and PATRICIA MAZZEI from New York; JESS BIDGOOD from Boston; and MITCH SMITH from Chicago.

National School Walkout: Thousands Protest Against Gun Violence Across the U.S.

BY VIVIAN YEE AND ALAN BLINDER | MARCH 14, 2018

A MONTH AGO, hundreds of teenagers ran for their lives from the hallways and classrooms of Marjory Stoneman Douglas High School, where 17 students and staff had been shot to death.

On Wednesday, driven by the conviction that they should never have to run from guns again, they walked.

So did their peers. In New York City, in Chicago, in Atlanta and Santa Monica; at Columbine High School and in Newtown, Conn.; and in many more cities and towns, students left school by the hundreds and the thousands at 10 a.m., sometimes in defiance of school authorities, who seemed divided and even flummoxed about how to handle their emptying classrooms.

The first major coordinated action of the student-led movement for gun control marshaled the same elements that had defined it ever since the Parkland shooting: eloquent young voices, equipped with symbolism and social media savvy, riding a resolve as yet untouched by cynicism.

"We have grown up watching more tragedies occur and continuously asking: Why?" said Kaylee Tyner, a 16-year-old junior at Columbine High School outside Denver, where 13 people were killed in 1999, inaugurating, in the public consciousness, the era of school shootings. "Why does this keep happening?"

Even after a year of near continuous protesting — for women, for the environment, for immigrants and more — the emergence of people not even old enough to drive as a political force has been particularly arresting, unsettling a gun control debate that had seemed impervious to other factors.

In Florida, where students from Stoneman Douglas High and other schools had rallied in the state capital, the governor signed a bill last week that raised the minimum age to purchase a firearm to 21 and extended the waiting period to three days.

On a national level, the students have not had the same impact. This week, President Trump abandoned gun control proposals that the Republican-led Congress had never even inched toward supporting.

But, for one day at least, the students commanded the country's airwaves, Twitter feeds and Snapchat stories.

Principals and superintendents seemed disinclined to stop them. Some were outright supportive, though others warned that students would face disciplinary consequences for leaving school. At many schools, teachers and parents joined in.

Wreathed in symbolism, the walkouts generally lasted for 17 minutes, one for each of the Parkland victims. Two more nationwide protests are set to take place on March 24 and on April 20, the anniversary of the Columbine shooting.

On a soccer field burned yellow by the Colorado sun, Ms. Tyner stood alongside hundreds of her fellow students, who waved signs — "This is our future," one said — and released red, white and blue balloons.

Yet in many places, for many students, Wednesday was just Wednesday, and class went on. Even at Columbine, the embrace of the gun control movement was not universal.

"People say it's all about gun control, it's all about, 'We should ban guns,' " said Caleb Conrad, 16, a junior, who stayed in class. "But that's not the real issue here. The real issue is the people who are doing it."

In the one-school rural community of Potosi, Wis., no student group had organized a protest. After a handful of students expressed some interest, the school decided to hold an assembly at 10 a.m. to talk about school safety measures and the value of being kind to one another.

Students walked out of Marjory Stoneman Douglas High School in Parkland, Fla., on Wednesday, one month after 17 people were killed in a shooting at the school.

At 10 a.m., one student, a female freshman, left the building alone.

Throughout the assembly, she sat by herself outside, by a flagpole, for 17 minutes. She appeared to be praying, said the principal, Mike Uppena, adding that she was not in trouble for leaving.

Officials in Lafayette Parish, La., initially said that students could participate in the day's events, believing that it was appropriate to honor the Florida victims. But when it became clear there was a political motive to the walkout, a torrent of complaints from the local community led the school board to adopt a new plan: a minute of silence.

Dozens of students walked out anyway.

OUT OF CLASS AND INTO THE STREETS

In some places, demonstrators chanted and held signs. At other schools, students stood in silence. In Atlanta, some students took a knee.

Thousands of New York City students converged on central locations — Columbus Circle, Battery Park, Brooklyn Borough Hall, Lincoln Center.

Gov. Andrew M. Cuomo, a Democrat, stretched out on the sidewalk as part of a "die-in" with students in Zuccotti Park in Lower Manhattan, the former home of the Occupy Wall Street protests.

Hundreds sat in the middle of West 62nd Street for several minutes before rising to their feet and shouting, "No more violence." A cry of "Trump Tower!" sent dozens of protesters marching toward the Trump International Hotel and Tower across Broadway. Onlookers gave them fist-bumps.

In Washington, thousands left their classrooms in the city and its suburbs and marched to the Capitol steps, their high-pitched voices battling against the stiff wind: "Hey-hey, ho-ho, the N.R.A. has got to go!" One sign said: "Fix This, Before I Text My Mom from Under A Desk."

Members of Congress, overwhelmingly Democratic, emerged from the Capitol to meet them. Trailed by aides and cameras, some legislators high-fived the children in the front rows, others took selfies, and nearly all soon learned that the young protesters had no idea who they were.

Except, of course, for "BERNIE SANDERS!" which the protesters screamed at the Vermont senator, as well at some other white-haired, bespectacled legislators.

Asked by reporters about the walkouts, Raj Shah, Mr. Trump's deputy press secretary, said the president "shares the students' concerns about school safety" and cited his support for mental health and background check improvements.

As the hours passed, the walkouts moved west across the country.

"It's 10 o'clock," said a man on the intercom at Perspectives Charter Schools on Chicago's South Side. With that, hundreds of students streamed out of their classrooms and into the neighborhood, marching past modest brick homes, a Walgreens and multiple churches.

Posters advertising the walkout at Perspectives Charter Schools in Chicago.

Several current and former Perspectives students have been killed in recent years, the school president said.

"You see different types of violence going on," said Armaria Broyles, a junior who helped lead the walkout and whose older brother was killed in a shooting. "We all want a good community and we all want to make a change."

At Santa Monica High School in Southern California, teachers guided hundreds of students to the football field. It felt like a cross between a political rally and pep rally, with dozens of students wearing orange T-shirts, the color of the gun control movement, and #neveragain scrawled onto their arms in black eyeliner.

"It is our duty to win," Roger Gawne, a freshman and one of the protest organizers, yelled to the crowd.

STAYING SILENT, FOR THE OPPOSITE REASON

Although the walkouts commanded attention on cable television and social media for much of Wednesday, it also was clear that many students did not participate, especially in rural and conservative areas where gun control is not popular.

At Bartlesville High School in Bartlesville, Okla., where hundreds of students walked out of class last month to protest cuts in state education funding, nothing at all happened at 10 a.m.

"I haven't heard a word about it," the principal, LaDonna Chancellor, said of the gun protest.

In Iowa, Russell Reiter, superintendent of the Oskaloosa Community School District, suggested that temperatures below 40 degrees may have encouraged students to stay indoors, but he also said that "students here are just not interested in what is going on in bigger cities."

There was opposition even in liberal Santa Monica. Just after the organizers of the walkout there read the names of the Parkland victims, another student went on stage, grabbed the microphone and shouted "Support the Second Amendment!" before he was called off by administrators.

'WE NEED MORE THAN JUST 17 MINUTES'

Some of the day's most poignant demonstrations happened at schools whose names are now synonymous with shootings.

Watched by a phalanx of reporters, camera operators and supporters, hundreds of students crowded onto the football field at Stoneman Douglas High shortly after 10 a.m.

A month after the Feb. 14 shooting, notes of condolence, fading flowers and stuffed toys, damp from recent rain, still lay on the grass outside the school and affixed to metal fences.

The walkout was allowed by the school, but several students said they were warned that they would not be permitted back onto the campus for the day if they left school grounds. Despite the warning, a couple of hundred students marched to a nearby park for another demonstration.

Students from Marjory Stoneman Douglas High School in Parkland, Fla., gathered at the nearby Pine Trails Park.

"We need more than just 17 minutes," Nicolle Montgomerie, 17, a junior, said as she walked toward the park.

An email from the school soon went out telling students they could return.

In Newtown, Conn., where 26 people were killed at Sandy Hook Elementary School in 2012, hundreds of students at Newtown High School gathered in a parking lot near the football field. Two hours later, it was Columbine's turn.

A WORD OR TWO FROM GUN RIGHTS GROUPS

Shortly after the walkouts began, the National Rifle Association said on Twitter, "Let's work together to secure our schools and stop school violence."

But the next tweet left no doubt as to where the N.R.A. stood on the message of the protests. It said, "I'll control my own guns, thank you.

Students rallied for gun control legislation in Manhattan on Wednesday.

#2A #NRA" atop a photo of an AR-15, the kind of high-powered rifle used at Stoneman Douglas High and in other mass shootings.

The Gun Owners of America, a smaller organization often seen as more militant than the N.R.A., was more defiant.

The group urged its supporters to call their elected officials to oppose gun control measures like Fix NICS, which is intended to improve reporting by state and federal agencies to the criminal background check system. "We could win or lose the gun control battle in the next 96 hours," the group said on Twitter.

The group also celebrated "the pro-gun students who are not supporting their anti-gun counterparts."

WARNINGS FROM SCHOOLS, NOT ALWAYS HEEDED

Some schools accommodated or even encouraged the protests. But others warned that they would mark students who left as absent, or even suspend them.

In Cobb County, Ga., near Atlanta, the threat of punishment did not keep scores of Walton High School students from standing in silence on the football field for 170 seconds. A school district spokesman did not respond to a request for comment on what would happen to the students.

Noelle Ellerson Ng, associate executive director for policy and advocacy for AASA, the association of the nation's superintendents, said that schools had to balance the First Amendment rights of students with their other responsibilities, including safety.

Indeed, several protests were canceled because of threats of the same kind of violence the students were demonstrating against. A demonstration at Broughton High School in Raleigh, N.C., was called off when the principal learned of what she later described as "a false rumor of a threat and a post on social media that caused unnecessary fear among our school community."

Reporting was contributed by **JESS BIDGOOD, JULIE BOSMAN, SYDNEY EMBER, DANA GOLDSTEIN, ANEMONA HARTOCOLLIS, SEAN KEENAN, NICK MADIGAN, JENNIFER MEDINA, JOHN PERAGINE, RICK ROJAS, STEPHANIE SAUL, NATE SCHWEBER, MITCH SMITH, KATE TAYLOR, JULIE TURKEWITZ** and **ELIZABETH WILLIAMSON**.

Students Lead Huge Rallies for Gun Control Across the U.S.

BY MICHAEL D. SHEAR | MARCH 24, 2018

WASHINGTON — Standing before vast crowds from Washington to Los Angeles to Parkland, Fla., the speakers — nearly all of them students, some still in elementary school — delivered an anguished and defiant message: They are "done hiding" from gun violence, and will "stop at nothing" to get politicians to finally prevent it.

The students, as they seized the nation's attention on Saturday with raised fists and tear-streaked faces, vowed that their grief about school shootings and their frustration with adults' inaction would power a new generation of political activism.

"If they continue to ignore us, to only pretend to listen, then we will take action where it counts," Delaney Tarr, a student at Marjory Stoneman Douglas High School in Parkland, where a gunman killed 17 people last month, told tens of thousands rallying in Washington. "We will take action every day in every way until they simply cannot ignore us any more."

For many of the young people, the Washington rally, called March for Our Lives, was their first act of protest and the beginning of a political awakening. But that awakening may be a rude one — lawmakers in Congress have largely disregarded their pleas for action on television and social media in the five weeks since the Parkland shooting.

That reality helped drive the Parkland survivors in Washington, as they led a crowd that filled blocks of Pennsylvania Avenue between the White House and Capitol Hill. Thousands more rallied at about 800 "sibling" marches around the country and abroad, where students, like those in the capital, made eloquent calls for gun control and pledged to exercise their newfound political power in the midterm elections this fall.

Aerial video captured seas of people — in front of Trump International Hotel in New York; in a central square in Tokyo; along the streets of Boston; at a rally in downtown Fort Worth, Tex.; and crammed into a park less than a mile from Stoneman Douglas High.

Delivered in soaring speeches, emotional chants and hand-painted signs, the protesters' messages offered angry rebukes to the National Rifle Association and politicians who have left gun laws largely intact for decades. A sign in Washington declared "Graduations, not funerals!" while another in New York said "I should be learning, not protesting." Crowds in Chicago chanted "Fear has no place in our schools" as they marched.

Celebrities, including Lin-Manuel Miranda, the "Hamilton" star, and the pop singers Ariana Grande and Miley Cyrus, performed in Washington, where politicians and adult activists were largely sidelined in favor of the fresh-faced students offering stories of fear and frustration, but also hope for change.

The most powerful, and impassioned, moments came from the surviving students of the Parkland shooting, who declared themselves angry, impatient and determined to stop the slaughter.

"Today, we march," Ms. Tarr said. "We fight. We roar. We prepare our signs. We raise them high. We know what we want, we know how to get it and we are not waiting any more."

An 11-year-old girl from Virginia, Naomi Wadler, captivated her audience as she declared "Never again!" on behalf of black women and girls who have been the victims of gun violence.

Calls like Naomi's stood in stark contrast to action on Capitol Hill and at the White House in the hours before the rallies. President Trump signed a $1.3 trillion spending bill that took no significant new steps on gun control: It did nothing to expand background checks, impose additional limits on assault weapons, require a higher age for rifle purchases or curb the sale of high-capacity ammunition magazines.

The spending legislation, which was viewed as the last opportunity this year for Congress to enact major new gun restrictions before the midterm elections in November, included only some school safety measures and modest improvements to the background check system.

Organizers at national gun control groups, who provided logistical support and public relations advice as the students planned the Washington rally, said they believed that the students would not become disillusioned by the lack of immediate action in Congress. They noted that rallies took place in 390 of the country's 435 congressional districts.

"The mass shooting generation is nearing voting age," said John Feinblatt, the president of Everytown for Gun Safety, a national group that advocates tougher gun laws. "They know the midterms are six months away, and they plan to make sure that they vote and they get others to register to vote. They are absolutely poised to turn this moment into a movement."

Gun rights organizations largely stayed silent on Saturday, following vigorous efforts since the Parkland shooting to squash any movement toward significant gun control legislation. A spokesman for the N.R.A. declined repeated requests for comment.

On the eve of the march, Colion Noir, a host on NRATV, an online video channel produced by the gun group, lashed out at the Parkland students, saying that "no one would know your names" if someone with a weapon had stopped the gunman at their school.

"These kids ought to be marching against their own hypocritical belief structures," he said in the video, adding: "The only reason we've ever heard of them is because the guns didn't come soon enough."

Small counterprotests took place in a few cities. In Salt Lake City, several hundred people gathered near a high school, some carrying signs with messages like "AR-15's EMPOWER the people." Brandon McKee, who wore a pistol on his belt, brought his daughter, Kendall, 11, who held a sign that said "Criminals love gun control."

"I believe it's their goal to unarm America, and that's why we're here today," Mr. McKee said of the Washington marchers. In Boston, about 20 protesters favoring gun control confronted a small clutch of Second Amendment supporters in front of the State House. The two sides quickly got into a shouting match.

The pro-gun protests were swamped in size and enthusiasm by those marching for gun control, many of whom traveled for many hours to attend the rallies in cities across the country. Sebastian Jennings, 18, said he spent 36 hours taking a bus to Washington from western Arkansas. Tour buses lined the streets.

Security was tight in Washington, where military trucks and guards blocked almost every intersection near the rally amid a huge police presence, and in other cities where marches and rallies forced the closing of major roads.

In towns like Dahlonega, Ga., smaller rallies sought to demonstrate a desire for new gun restrictions even in rural, Republican-leaning communities where gun ownership is common and support for the Second Amendment is strong.

"We're going to be the generation that takes down the gun lobby," Marisa Pyle, 20, said through a red megaphone to a group of several hundred people gathered in front of the Dahlonega Gold Museum.

Around the world, Americans living abroad gathered to honor those who have died in school shootings and to echo the call for gun control.

Protesters in Rome jammed the sidewalk across from the American Embassy, next to the upscale Via Veneto, raising their voice in chants — "Hey hey, ho ho, the N.R.A. has got to go," and waving signs with messages like "A gun is not fun" and "Am I next?" many made by high school students at an international school.

About 150 to 200 people in Berlin gathered in solidarity in front of the Brandenburg Gate, just steps from the American Embassy. Many carried hand-painted signs, among them: "Arms should be for hugging," "Bullets aren't school supplies" and "Waffeln statt Waffen" (Waffles instead of weapons).

One of the largest rallies outside Washington was at a Florida park not far from Stoneman Douglas High School. During that event, 17 students from the school silently took the stage to represent their friends who had been killed.

Anthony Montalto, the brother of Gina Rose Montalto, one of those killed, held a sign that said: "My sister could not make it here today. I'm here for her."

"Turn this moment into a movement," Sari Kaufman, a sophomore at Stoneman Douglas, implored the sea of students, parents and teachers. She urged her classmates to vote out of office politicians who receive money from the N.R.A. "They think we're all talk and no action."

But the largest rally, by far, was in Washington, where stage risers and giant television monitors were set up in the shadow of the Capitol — the focus of much of the anger from students throughout the day.

One protester carried a sign that said "If the opposite of pro is con, then the opposite of progress is Congress."

Most Republican and Democratic members of Congress had already left the city to return to their home districts for spring break. Mr. Trump spent Saturday afternoon in Florida, at the Trump International Golf Club, less than an hour north of Parkland. A White House spokeswoman said in a statement, "We applaud the many courageous young Americans exercising their First Amendment rights today."

City officials had prepared for the biggest march since about a half-million women gathered on the day after Mr. Trump's inauguration, declaring a new political movement aimed at resisting the president and his policies.

On Saturday, officials with Metro, the region's subway system, said more than 207,000 rides had been taken on the system by 1 p.m., about half of the number by that time during the Women's March.

A team of crowd science researchers led by G. Keith Still of Manchester Metropolitan University in England estimated that about 180,000 people attended the rally. They examined photographs, video and satellite imagery to estimate the crowd density in different areas of the demonstration. The number is less than half of the 470,000 that Dr. Still estimated had attended the Women's March in Washington in 2017.

Even so, the streets of Washington were packed on Saturday. Teenagers climbed on each other's shoulders to reach the bare limbs of trees, where they climbed higher. And each student who spoke drew a cheer that matched, and even eclipsed, the applause given to the musical performers.

Edna Chavez, 17, a high school senior from Los Angeles, said she had lost her brother to gun violence: "He was in high school when he passed away. It was a day like any other day. Sunset down on South Central. You hear pops, thinking they're fireworks."

"Ricardo was his name. Can you all say it with me?" she asked. The crowd said his name over and over again, as Ms. Chavez smiled through tears.

Naomi Wadler, the 11-year-old student, introduced herself with a soft "hi" and said she represented the black women who have been victims of gun violence.

"People have said that I am too young to have these thoughts on my own," she said. "People have said that I am a tool of some nameless adult. It's not true. My friends and I might still be 11, and we might still be in elementary school, but we know."

She added, "And we know that we have seven short years until we, too, have the right to vote."

Reporting was contributed by EMILY BAUMGAERTNER, EMILY COCHRANE, SABRINA TAVERNISE, PATRICIA MAZZEI and NOAH WEILAND from Washington; JILL BURKE from Anchorage; JEFF MAYS, ANNIE CORREAL, JACEY FORTIN and JONATHAN WOLFE from New York; ALAN BLINDER from Dahlonega, Ga.; MITCH SMITH from Chicago; JULIE TURKEWITZ from Salt Lake City; NICK MADIGAN from Parkland, Fla.; JOSE DEL REAL from Los Angeles; JESS BIDGOOD from Montpelier, Vt.; MARK LANDLER from Palm Beach, Fla.; CHRISTOPHER SCHUETZE from Berlin; ELISABETTA POVOLEDO from Rome; and HISAKO UENO from Tokyo.

For Parkland Students, a Surreal Journey From 'Normal' to a Worldwide March

BY PATRICIA MAZZEI | MARCH 24, 2018

WASHINGTON — Little has returned to normal for the students of Marjory Stoneman Douglas High School since Feb. 14, when a gunman killed 14 of their classmates and three staff members.

They juggle homework with activism. They wince at loud noises. Sometimes, they sleep.

But to the huge crowds that greeted them in Washington on Saturday at a march to protest gun violence, the students were fearless celebrities.

"We're here for you, Douglas!" a girl shrieked as five teenage boys from Stoneman Douglas and their history teacher made their way to the main stage.

"Go Douglas!" said the teacher, Greg Pittman.

As the crowd broke into applause, the boys remained stoic. They held up their poster boards — "It is a school zone, not a war zone," read one — and looked straight ahead.

They were part of a group of 200 people from Stoneman Douglas, in Parkland, Fla., who were sponsored by Giffords, the gun control advocacy group, to come to the Washington march. An alumni group raised enough money to get more than 550 additional students to the rally, a spokeswoman for the group said. Others traveled to Washington on their own, some of them rooming with family and friends.

Despite their numbers, their steady presence in the news, their unmistakable influence on the national debate over guns, some of them were trying to be teenagers again.

It hasn't been easy.

The five boys did not organize the event on Saturday, called the March for Our Lives. They did not lose a relative in the shooting. They were not injured.

But their coach, Aaron Feis, was killed. Their school was forever changed. And now, they were in the nation's capital, feeling hundreds of eyes on them as they walked down Constitution Avenue.

"There's a lot of emotion," said one, Adrian Kauffman, 16.

The five boys, all sophomores, refrained from endorsing a specific policy proposal or calling out politicians they dislike. They arrived to show strength in numbers, "so nothing like this happens again," said Adam Hostig, 15.

"Most teenagers talk about drama about girlfriends and boyfriends," said Zach Cooper, 16. "And we're talking about bomb threats and guns."

"Nonstop," Adam said.

A police helicopter hovered overhead. Adam's eyes darted up suspiciously.

"Even coming to an event like this, it's scary," Zach said.

None of them paid much attention to the politics of guns before the shooting, they admitted. "We got more informed," said Evan Kuperman, 16.

The march will make it "feel like the people who died did not die in vain," added Josh Funk, 16.

Amid their newfound activism, they have tried to return to lives that resemble those they had before their high school turned into a mass-murder scene.

"You get a sense of guilt trying to have fun," Josh said. "But at the same time, you just want to be with friends and family all the time. To never miss a moment."

In Washington this week, the Florida visitors sponsored by Giffords went to museums and shared late-night ice cream sundaes in a hotel ballroom with foosball tables and a Pac-Man machine.

But they also roved the hallways of the Capitol, meeting with lawmakers and lobbying for action on gun violence. The House minority leader, Nancy Pelosi, dropped in on their hotel. Some of them met former Vice President Joe Biden.

"I've gotten about nine hours of sleep in four days," Aly Sheehy, an 18-year-old senior, said near midnight on Friday. "But being around other people that understand what I've gone through just recharges me."

"On Sunday, we'll all be exhausted," she added. "But then we'll go back. For something this important, I'll make the time."

"They definitely think we're going to go away," Jose Iglesias, a 17-year-old senior, said of politicians and skeptical adults. "We know what we're doing. We have tactics. They think we're just children."

The students knew that interest in their cause might fade outside their own schools. They knew that for the grown-ups, the march, which was organized in a little more than a month, might seem like the culmination of their efforts. "It's just the beginning," Jose said.

On Saturday morning, he awoke early. "In my sleep, I called 911," he said. "Really it was my alarm that kept going off."

"I have flashbacks of running into a classroom," said Sarah Pierre, 17, a senior.

Over breakfast, students made last-minute signs with Crayola markers. Natasha Martinez, a 17-year-old junior, got on FaceTime with her mother, who was attending the march back home in Parkland. Her mother worried that Natasha was underdressed for the Washington cold. "I'm wearing the thermal, a turtleneck, this hoodie I bought, and a coat," Natasha insisted.

A friend sitting next to her, Isabel Chequer, a 16-year-old junior, waved at Natasha's mother.

"She has a special pass," Natasha said, pointing at Isabel's neck. "Injured club!" said Isabel, who was twice grazed during the shooting. She was one of 17 people hurt.

Isabel fears the shooting will make it impossible for her to watch action movies anymore, despite her interest in film.

"I feel like I can't see those movies again, like 'Black Panther' or

Chloe Trieu, 15, center, a student at Stoneman Douglas, and her sister Victoria, 19, an alumna of the school, at the march.

'Annihilation,' which makes me really sad, because I love movies so much," she said. "It's taken a little bit from myself."

"I feel weird doing normal things," her schoolmate Aly said.

Throngs of marchers soon took to the streets downtown. Students from Stoneman Douglas and other schools delivered speeches, some choked with emotion as they described living with violent memories, survivor's guilt and the ever-present shadow of fear.

Samantha Fuentes, an 18-year-old senior who was shot in both legs during the shooting, went on stage to read a poem.

Halfway through it, she appeared to get nervous and quickly ducked behind the podium. She stood back up as people rushed from backstage to help her. "I just threw up on international television, and it feels great," she said with a laugh, before reading the rest of her poem.

It ended: "Will you give up? Or is enough enough?"

When the speeches — along with performances by Ariana Grande, Miley Cyrus and others — were finished, and the crowds began to disperse, the Stoneman Douglas students became tourists again, albeit ones who had moved thousands.

Amanda Lee, a 17-year-old junior who had been in one of the classrooms where shots were fired, left the rally with other students, pausing to snap pictures of the cherry blossoms that had started to bloom along the street.

Amanda said she had expected more of an actual march than speeches and a concert. But the magnitude of what they had accomplished in less than two months, she said, hit when she saw images of protests across the country and around the world.

"It sinks in," she said. "And then you feel that you've done the impossible."

EMILY COCHRANE contributed reporting from Washington and **JACEY FORTIN** from New York.

March for Our Lives Highlights: Students Protesting Guns Say 'Enough Is Enough'

BY THE NEW YORK TIMES | MARCH 24, 2018

DEMONSTRATORS FLOODED STREETS across the globe in public protests on Saturday, calling for action against gun violence. Hundreds of thousands of marchers turned out, in the most ambitious show of force yet from a student-driven movement that emerged after the recent massacre at a South Florida high school.

At the main event in Washington, survivors of mass shootings, including the one in Florida, rallied a whooping crowd — "Welcome to the revolution," said one of the student organizers — and spoke of communities that are disproportionately affected by gun violence. "It is normal to see flowers honoring the lives of black and brown youth that have lost their lives to a bullet," Edna Chavez, 17, said of her South Los Angeles neighborhood.

• In New York, marchers bundled in bright orange — the official color of a gun control advocacy group — charged toward Central Park. And in Parkland, Fla., less than a mile from where the shooting took place last month, one protester's eyes brimmed with tears, surrounded by the echoing chant, "Enough is enough!"

• Small groups of counterprotesters supporting gun rights also marched in different cities. In Salt Lake City, demonstrators carried pistols and flags. One of their signs read: "What can we do to stop mass shootings? SHOOT BACK." In Boston, opposing groups of protesters shouted at one another before the police intervened.

• More than 800 protests were planned in every American state, including in some gun-friendly cities, and on every continent except for Antarctica, according to a website set up by organizers.

• Planning for the events was spearheaded by a group of students from Marjory Stoneman Douglas High School in Parkland, Fla., who have emerged as national anti-gun figures in the wake of the shooting that left 17 dead.

• Sharp-tongued and defiant, the student leaders hoped to elevate gun control as a key issue during the upcoming midterm elections, and to inspire their peers to register to vote en masse.

• They were building on the success of a national school walkout this month, and gun control legislation in Florida that they helped to usher in. Their goal remains, as articulated online in the event's mission statement, to "demand that a comprehensive and effective bill be immediately brought before Congress to address these gun issues."

• The White House responded to the demonstrations in a statement. "We applaud the many courageous young Americans exercising their First Amendment rights today," it read. On Friday, the Justice Department proposed banning so-called bump stocks, but President Trump signed a spending bill that included only some background checks and school safety measures.

• The Times had journalists covering the marches in Washington; New York; Boston; Montpelier, Vt.; Parkland, Fla; Dahlonega, Ga.; Chicago; Salt Lake City; Los Angeles; Seattle; Anchorage, Alaska; Rome; Berlin; and Tokyo.

THE STUDENT ORGANIZERS WANT ACTION IN A MIDTERM YEAR.

The student activists emphasized that they would soon have access to the ballot box as they hope to build support for candidates who support universal background checks and bans on assault-style weapons.

Participants in New York City walking through Columbus Circle on Saturday.

Large majorities of Americans say they support gun control measures like universal background checks. Yet when put directly to the people in a referendum in recent years, the results have been mixed.

At street intersections in Washington on Saturday, voter registration volunteers waved clipboards over their heads, shouting, "It takes less than three minutes!" They wore neon yellow shirts that read, "Register to vote!"

"These Parkland students have already been able to make change that no one else could for decades," said Carol Williams, a volunteer from West Chester, Pa.

In Parkland on Saturday, Sari Kaufman, a Stoneman Douglas sophomore, urged people to "turn this moment into a movement" that would push out of office any politician who took money from the National Rifle Association.

"They think we're all talk and no action," she said to loud applause and cheers, and urged the crowd to prove politicians wrong by voting in huge numbers.

"Remember that policy change is not nearly as difficult as losing a loved one," she said. "Don't just go out and vote: Get 17 other people to go out and vote."

The crowd was particularly rousing in its appreciation of Casey Sherman, 17, a Douglas student and one of the Parkland rally organizers.

"My love for Parkland had taken on a whole new meaning," she said. "After all this heartbreak, we have come back stronger than ever. Those 17 people did not die in vain. We will stop at nothing until we make real, lasting change."

'WELCOME TO THE REVOLUTION,' ONE OF THE STUDENT ORGANIZERS SAID IN WASHINGTON.

At the rally in Washington, the first speaker was Cameron Kasky, 17, a junior at Stoneman Douglas who last month challenged Senator Marco Rubio of Florida, a Republican, to stop accepting donations from the National Rifle Association. Mr. Kasky called for universal background checks on gun sales and a ban on assault rifles.

"To the leaders, skeptics and cynics who told us to sit down and stay silent: Wait your turn," Mr. Kasky said. "Welcome to the revolution."

Another speaker, Edna Chavez, 17, a high school senior in Los Angeles, said she had lost her brother to gun violence. "Ricardo was his name. Can you all say it with me?" she asked.

The crowd said his name over and over again, as Ms. Chavez smiled through tears.

Alex Wind, 17, a junior at Stoneman Douglas, spoke about the need for legislative change.

"To all the politicians out there, if you take money from the N.R.A., you have chosen death," he said. "If you have not expressed to your constituents a public stance on this issue, you have chosen death. If you do not stand with us by saying we need to pass common sense

ERIN SCHAFF FOR THE NEW YORK TIMES

Jada Wright, 17, a student at Eastern Senior High School, cries during the March for Our Lives rally in Washington on Saturday.

gun legislation, you have chosen death. And none of the millions of people marching in this country today will stop until they see those against us out of office, because we choose life."

David Hogg, 17, a senior at the high school and one of the most recognizable faces of the movement, said: "Who here is going to vote in the 2018 election? If you listen real close, you can hear the people in power shaking."

On Saturday, officials with Metro, the region's subway system, said more than 207,000 rides had been taken on the system by 1 p.m., about half of the number by that time during the women's march.

A team of crowd science researchers led by the professor G. Keith Still of Manchester Metropolitan University in England estimated that about 180,000 people attended Saturday's rally in Washington. They examined photographs, video and satellite imagery of the rally to estimate the crowd density in different areas of the demonstration.

The number is less than half of the 470,000 that Mr. Still estimated had attended the women's march in Washington in 2017.

EMMA GONZÁLEZ, ONE OF THE STUDENT ORGANIZERS, STOOD FOR SEVERAL MINUTES OF SILENCE.

Ms. González spoke for just under two minutes on Saturday at the rally in Washington, describing the effects of gun violence in emotional detail and reciting the names of classmates who had been killed.

Then she said nothing for four minutes and 26 seconds.

She stared straight ahead during her period of silence onstage, her sometimes watery eyes fixed in the distance. Then a timer went off.

"Since the time that I came out here, it has been six minutes and 20 seconds," she said. "The shooter has ceased shooting, and will soon abandon his rifle, blend in with the students as they escape, and walk free for an hour before arrest.

"Fight for your lives, before it's someone else's job," she continued, and then walked offstage.

IN NEW YORK, 150,000 PEOPLE WERE MARCHING, THE MAYOR SAID.

In New York, Mayor Bill de Blasio said early in the afternoon on Twitter that an estimated 150,000 people were marching. "You have to know when a revolution is starting," he said.

The musician Paul McCartney, speaking to CNN at the march, opened his jacket to show a T-shirt that read "We can end gun violence."

"This is what we can do, so I'm here to do it," Mr. McCartney said. "One of my best friends was killed in gun violence right around here, so it's important to me," he added, referring to his Beatles bandmate John Lennon, who was shot and killed in December 1980 outside his apartment on the Upper West Side.

As the crowd thickened before a rally in front of the Trump International Hotel and Tower near Columbus Circle, Mary Ann Jacobs,

The March for Our Lives in New York City on Saturday.

55, of Sandy Hook, Conn., milled in the crowd with her husband.

Ms. Jacobs was a library clerk during the massacre at Sandy Hook Elementary School. She barricaded herself in the school's library, "in a closet hidden behind file cabinets" along with 18 fourth graders.

"In the months after the shooting it took 100 percent of my personal focus to get up and go to work every day to take care of my surviving students," she said.

OPPONENTS OF GUN CONTROL STAGED THEIR OWN SMALLER RALLIES IN BOSTON AND SALT LAKE CITY.
Tensions over guns seemed to converge in Salt Lake City, where a gun rights march kicked off just minutes before a gun control march.

The gun rights rally drew hundreds of people, many carrying signs — "AR-15s EMPOWER the people," one said.

Brandon McKee was one of the many people with pistols on their hips. His daughter Kendall, 11, held a sign: "Criminals love gun control."

Demonstrators at a gun rights rally in Salt Lake City on Saturday. It was one of several such counterdemonstrations across the country as hundreds of thousands marched in support of gun control.

Mr. McKee said of the Washington marchers: "I believe it's their goal to unarm America, and that's why we're here today. We're not going to stand idly by and let them tell us what we can and cannot do."

As the gun rights advocates set off toward the Capitol, some began to heckle a gun control advocate, Linda Peer, 67, who had infiltrated the march line.

"She's not a true American!" one man yelled. "Shame on you!" the group chanted at her.

In Boston, a clutch of Second Amendment supporters gathered in front of the Statehouse with signs that said, "Come and take it."

"We believe in the Second Amendment," said Paul Allen, 62, a retired construction worker who lives in Salisbury, Mass. "You people will interpret it the way you want and we'll interpret it for what it is —

that law-abiding citizens who are true patriots have the right to bear arms."

Mr. Allen described supporters of gun control as "ignorant sheep who are being spoon-fed by liberal teachers."

"They haven't read the Constitution and they don't know what it means," he said.

Gun rights organizations were mostly quiet about the demonstrations on Saturday. A spokesman for the N.R.A. did not answer several emails requesting comment.

On the eve of the march, Colion Noir, a host on NRATV, an online video channel produced by the gun group, lashed out at the Parkland students, saying that "no one would know your names" if someone with a weapon had stopped the gunman at their school.

"These kids ought to be marching against their own hypocritical belief structures," he said in the video, adding, "The only reason we've ever heard of them is because the guns didn't come soon enough."

DEMONSTRATORS GATHERED IN GUN-FRIENDLY STATES.

In places where gun control is less popular, demonstrators pooled together, trying to show that support for their cause extends beyond large, predominantly liberal cities.

In Vermont, a rural state with a rich hunting culture and some of the nation's weakest gun laws, marchers gathered at the Capitol in Montpelier. Organizers hoped that thousands would turn out by the end of the day — an ambitious goal in a city of 7,500 people.

"I hope the national march is going to be impactful, but at least we know state by state that we can make change," said Madison Knoop, a college freshman who organized the rally.

In Dahlonega, Ga., several hundred people gathered outside a museum, a surprising show of strength for gun control in an overwhelmingly conservative region.

"We're going to be the generation that takes down the gun lobby," Marisa Pyle, 20, said through a megaphone.

Ms. Pyle, a student at the University of Georgia and an organizer of Saturday's rally in Lumpkin County, challenged critics of the demonstrations across the country.

"I'm starting to think they just want to shut us up because they're scared of what we have to say," Ms. Pyle said.

Young people were scattered in a crowd dominated by people in middle age and older. There were few signs of counterprotesters. But as Ms. Pyle led a roll call of the Stoneman Douglas victims, a man in a passing vehicle yelled: "Trump! Trump! Trump!"

In Anchorage, the largest city in Alaska, marchers gathered in weather that peaked above freezing around noon.

Alaska has not seen a school shooting in two decades, but it has the highest rates of both gun-related deaths and suicides in the nation.

High schoolers turned out in jean jackets and hoodies, and shoveled snow to clear paths for one another in the 24-degree weather.

"Do you know how it feels to have the principal pretend over the intercom that the shooter is walking your way?" Elsa Hoppenworth, a 16-year-old junior at West Anchorage High School, asked a cheering crowd. "Those who do not contribute to change contribute to our death."

Melanie Anderson, a 44-year-old middle school teacher, held up a sign that said "teacher, not sharp shooter."

Keenly aware that Alaska is a pro-gun state, the students who marched and made speeches were careful to make clear that they were seeking modest reinforcements on existing gun laws, rather than all-out bans.

THE MESSAGE RESONATED FOR CHICAGO RESIDENTS ALL TOO FAMILIAR WITH GUN VIOLENCE.
Thousands of demonstrators came together at Chicago's Union Park, where speaker after speaker rattled off grim statistics about the city's endemic violence.

"Chicago has been plagued with gun violence way before the Parkland shooting," said Juan Reyes, a high school student. "Suddenly, people are talking about students not feeling safe in schools. But in reality, students in our city's South and West Sides have never felt safe."

Speaking at the rally in Washington, Trevon Bosley, a 19-year-old Chicago resident whose older brother Terrell died of a gunshot wound in 2006, said, "We deserve the right to have a life without fear of being gunned down."

Mya Middleton, 16, also traveled to speak in Washington, where she recalled an encounter with an armed man who was stealing from a store when she was a high school freshman.

"He pulls out this silver pistol and points it in my face and said these words that to this day haunt me and give me nightmares. He said, 'If you say anything, I will find you.' And yet I'm still saying something today," she said, to loud cheers.

AMERICANS IN TOKYO, ROME, MADRID AND BERLIN SHOWED SUPPORT.

On Saturday in Tokyo, where guns are highly restricted and shootings are rare, dozens of protesters gathered with signs bearing the names of people who have been killed by gun violence. Participants, many of them American, took turns reading poems or sharing memories of family members or friends killed in shootings.

"I think it is important not just to call for changes to our gun laws, not just to debate the subtleties of the Second Amendment, but to remember that it is people who have died because of our gun laws," said Linda Gould, an American in Japan who organized the vigil.

And in Nagoya, Japan, Mieko Hattori, the mother of Yoshihiro Hattori, a Japanese exchange student who was shot and killed in Baton Rouge, La., in the early 1990s, said earlier in the week, "I just wanted to convey our message: We support you from Japan."

In Rome on Saturday, demonstrators at the American Embassy chanted, "Hey hey, ho ho, the N.R.A. has got to go" and waved signs that read, "A Gun Is Not Fun" and "Am I Next?" The speakers at the rally included local students as well as Valentina and Gabriela Zuniga, a freshman and junior at Stoneman Douglas, who were on spring break.

"We knew there were rallies all over the world, and we looked for one in Rome," said Gabriela, 16, adding that her life had changed drastically since the shooting. "You go into class and see empty desks. It's different for everyone now."

Near the Brandenburg Gate in Berlin, 150 to 200 people, most of them Americans, held signs saying "bullets aren't school supplies" and "Waffeln statt Waffen" (Waffles Instead of Weapons).

Dylan von Felbert, 16, an 11th grader at the John F. Kennedy School in Berlin, said, "Our generation can be very apathetic — myself included — so I think it's important to support those things you really believe in."

In Madrid, a small crowd — almost all of them Americans — braved a cold Saturday to gather in front of the American embassy. An American student read out a list of all the American school shootings since the Columbine massacre.

Fiona Maharg Bravo attended with her 13-year-old daughter, Elena. Ms. Maharg Bravo grew up in Chicago but has lived in Madrid for more than 10 years.

"It's perhaps hard for people here to relate to what unfortunately is a uniquely American issue," she said.

Reporting was contributed by **ANNIE CORREAL**, **CAITLIN DICKERSON**, **JACEY FORTIN**, **JONATHAN WOLFE** and **LOUIS LUCERO II** from New York; **EMILY BAUMGAERTNER**, **EMILY COCHRANE**, **PATRICIA MAZZEI**, **SABRINA TAVERNISE** and **MICHAEL D. SHEAR** from Washington; **NICK MADIGAN** from Parkland, Fla.; **JULIE TURKEWITZ** from Salt Lake City and Denver; **MITCH SMITH** from Chicago; **KATHARINE Q. SEELYE** from Boston; **JESS BIDGOOD** from Montpelier, Vt.; **ALAN BLINDER** from Dahlonega, Ga.; **JOSE A. DEL REAL** from Los Angeles; **JILL BURKE** from Anchorage, Alaska; **ELISABETTA POVOLEDO** from Rome; **CHRISTOPHER SCHUETZE** from Berlin; **RAPHAEL MINDER** from Madrid; and **HISAKO UENO** from Tokyo.

At Rallies, Students With a Different View of Gun Violence: As Urban Reality

BY NOAH WEILAND | MARCH 24, 2018

WASHINGTON — Sprinkled amid the throngs of young people protesting gun violence in Washington on Saturday were groups of students without signs denouncing President Trump, or the National Rifle Association, or the shooting massacres that have plagued the nation.

Instead, they carried megaphones and wore T-shirts calling attention to something close and constant: urban gun violence.

In cities such as Baltimore, the anguish of shootings feels different — the bloodshed comes not in isolated bursts of mass slaughter, but instead in a ceaseless rhythm, something that happens to friends and family, classmates and neighbors, in front yards and on playgrounds.

"In the inner city, there's a game: gunshots or firecrackers?" said Steve Sias, a high school student at Baltimore City College who came to the Washington march. "Whenever you hear the sound, you ask everyone in the house: Is it gunshots or firecrackers? Usually the parents say firecrackers so they don't startle the kids. But more times than not it's actually gunshots in the distance, or right outside your window."

Last year, Baltimore set a per capita record for homicides: 343 total, or about 56 for every 100,000 people. The city's population is just over 600,000. Its murder rate was by far the highest among the nation's 30 largest cities.

Students from Baltimore, as well as young people who attended a rally in Chicago, were vocal on Saturday about the need for steps to reduce gun violence, much in the same way as students from Marjory Stoneman Douglas High School in Parkland, Fla., where a gunman killed 17 people last month. But they had a different idea of the problem.

Carrie Zaremba, left, Destini Philpot and Steve Sias, students from Baltimore, attended the March for Our Lives rally in Washington on Saturday.

Destini Philpot, another student at Baltimore City College, was joined on Saturday in Washington by Carrie Zaremba, a student at the Friends School of Baltimore, a predominantly white Quaker institution. The two said they had helped organize a citywide walkout this month that involved both public and private schools.

"It shouldn't take a mass shooting in a predominantly white area like Parkland to start caring about gun violence," Ms. Zaremba said.

Ms. Philpot said that many of those at the rally were thinking of gun violence in the only way they knew how: as mass shootings.

"When they talk about gun violence, they're talking about schools," she said.

Private donors paid for 60 buses that carried around 3,000 Baltimore students to the Washington event. Some Baltimore organizers skipped their city's satellite march to attend the one in the capital, hoping to reach an audience largely unfamiliar with the kind of violence that visits them with gruesome regularity.

One of those organizers, Erricka Bridgeford, has helped work on a campaign called Baltimore Ceasefire, which holds quarterly "ceasefire" weekends that call for a stop to killings for a three-day period.

On Saturday, she recalled what had brought her to Washington: the lasting agony from losing her brother, stepson and friends to gun violence.

"I've seen dead bodies and blood," she said. "These are things you never recover from. You learn how to live your life differently, because the air looks different once you experience that kind of trauma. I have to do something with the pain. I don't want to be a prisoner to it."

Ms. Bridgeford said shootings were a never-ending feature of life in her Baltimore neighborhood.

"There's no such thing as post-traumatic stress in a lot of communities in America, because there's no 'post,' " she said. "You don't get a chance to experience the aftermath before there's another trauma because of gun violence."

One of the students walking with Ms. Bridgeford was Shanika Walker, who attends the Excel Academy at Francis M. Wood High School in Baltimore, which recently lost seven students to homicide in 15 months.

"Only the scared people have guns, and they kill people they're scared of," she said. "There's a lot of fear."

On Chicago's Near West Side on Saturday, just a few miles from neighborhoods where shootings are common, thousands filled Union Park to protest a problem just as local.

Many came to the rally bearing personal stories of tragedy and loss, years of frustration with unchanged gun laws and hope replenished by recent student-led activism.

"We have been fighting for a long, long time," said Maria Pike, whose son, Ricky, 24, was shot to death in 2012. "And their voice is a fresh voice, is a true voice, is a transparent voice. And it comes from the heart."

Speaker after speaker at the Chicago rally mentioned relatives or classmates who had been wounded or killed in shootings, frustrated that past calls to action had not led to change.

"Chicago has been plagued with gun violence way before the Parkland shooting," said Juan Reyes, a high school student. "Suddenly, people are talking about students not feeling safe in schools. But in reality, students in our city's South and West Sides have never felt safe."

One high school student, Denzel Russell, told the crowd, "I have watched one of my friends get murdered while we were playing on the basketball court. That experience had me frozen and speechless."

Mr. Russell added: "We can come together for a march. But are we willing to come together to take action?"

Emerson Toomey, 17, who helped organize the Chicago march, said her mother was grazed by a bullet in a drive-by shooting on the North Side of the city.

"It's more about the journey to school for some kids than it is about the actual day at school," she said.

But for the teachers who believe they must now think as much about school shootings as they do about urban gun violence, Saturday's rallies in Washington and Chicago felt like the meeting of two threats, now inseparable.

"I see the look on the students' faces," said Jeremy McConnell, a special education teacher at Paul Laurence Dunbar High School in Baltimore. "They come from these communities. They come from these families that engage in this kind of violence. They might be a sibling or neighbor removed."

"They know gun violence is real. They see it in the streets," added Mr. McConnell, who, as the voice behind public address announcements at the school, reminds students to be vigilant after news of shootings in Baltimore and across the country. "But they haven't seen it in school. They think any day now it's coming here."

MITCH SMITH contributed reporting from Chicago.

Emboldened by Parkland, Newtown Students Find Their Voice

BY KRISTIN HUSSEY | AUG. 26, 2018

NEWTOWN, CONN. — Last year, Natalie Barden heard an announcement about a meeting of the Junior Newtown Action Alliance, a club for high school students working to reduce gun violence.

Natalie, who is 16 and about to start her junior year on Monday, knew of the club, but didn't know much about it. The announcement caught her attention. "I was like, 'Well, why am I not in that club?' " she said, perched on a stool in her family's kitchen in the village of Sandy Hook last week.

Natalie's parents, Mark and Jackie Barden, have been active in gun violence prevention since their 7-year-old son, Daniel, was killed. Daniel was one of 20 first graders and six educators shot to death at Sandy Hook Elementary School in 2012.

More than five years after the Sandy Hook massacre, the first-grade students who survived are 11- and 12-year-olds entering seventh grade in middle school.

But there were 400 other students in the school the day of the shootings. The oldest — fourth graders at the time — are now in high school, and have gradually begun to realize the power they wield by speaking out. And in increasing numbers, Newtown's teenagers are joining a network of young activists around the country who say they have had enough.

Those students remember the hourslong lockdown on Dec. 14, 2012. They knew something terrible had happened, but they did not know exactly what. They did not know if they were safe, or if they would see their families again.

Last fall, Natalie joined a handful of students at the first meeting of the Junior Newtown Action Alliance club, run by two seniors, Jackson Mittleman and Tommy Murray. She felt a little uncomfortable,

From the left, Tommy Murray, Jackson Mittleman, Natalie Barden and Jordan Gomes in front of a barn with the date of the 2012 Sandy Hook Elementary School shooting in Newtown, Conn. Natalie's brother Daniel was killed that day.

she said — talking about guns and shootings and death is emotionally draining for a teenager who lost her brother in the Sandy Hook massacre. But she stuck with it.

The club had struggled to attract members; at times just a few students showed up to meetings, Jackson and Tommy said. (Tommy Murray's mother, Po Murray, founded the Newtown Action Alliance after the shootings, and her children have been active in the junior club.)

In February, when 17 people were gunned down at Marjory Stoneman Douglas High School in Parkland, Fla., Natalie said she knew she needed to take decisive steps. "I decided that I just needed to do more," she said.

Natalie was not alone. About 100 students attended the Newtown High School club's next meeting. Jackson and Tommy watched as the room filled. With a newly energized membership, they quickly delegated jobs. One early focus was finding ways to increase their presence on social media to bring attention to their activism and to educate other teenagers. A club member started an Instagram account called HumansOfNewtownCT that features people telling their own stories.

In Parkland, students took to the national stage almost immediately. They began lobbying lawmakers to tighten Florida's gun laws and planned a coast-to-coast day of protests centered around the March for Our Lives in Washington that boosted activism among teenagers nationwide, including those touched by the Sandy Hook violence.

"That was definitely inspiring for me," Natalie said. If the Parkland students could mobilize so quickly to demand change, even as their wounds were fresh, Natalie said she realized it was her turn, too.

"I should be able to, five years later, use my voice in that way as well," Natalie said. She began talking with reporters who called, attended a Vogue Teen summit to talk about guns and wrote about her family's loss.

The students in Connecticut began focusing on organizing voter-registration drives and encouraging their peers to vote for candidates who support stricter gun laws, a Newtown student and activist, Jenny Wadhwa, said in an essay for Vice last spring. "What people need to realize is that we're not scared of mental illness or unarmed guards," she wrote. "We're scared of guns and inaction."

Among the Newtown group's goals: banning semiautomatic magazines that can hold dozens of bullets; closing loopholes in background check laws; and providing a route for courts and law enforcement to temporarily remove guns from people who pose a threat to themselves or others.

Newtown itself has shied away from its unwanted role as the poster child of mass school shootings.

Sandy Hook Elementary School was demolished months after the killings. Town leaders have encouraged the media to stay away on anniversaries, pleading for privacy. Students say teachers stick to a normal schedule each Dec. 14, as if it were a typical day.

Clockwise from top left, Natalie, Tommy, Jordan and Jackson.

But earlier this month, students from Parkland and teenagers who had joined the Road to Change bus tour as it crossed the country arrived in Newtown, their final stop. Ending their tour in Newtown felt important, said Jaclyn Corin, a student at Marjory Stoneman Douglas High School. "Unfortunately, Newtown and Parkland are forever connected," Jaclyn said.

The tour had included discussions with teenagers and victims of gun violence around the country, in city neighborhoods and in communities such as Aurora, Colo., and Las Vegas, the scenes of other mass shootings.

"I didn't know the strength of my voice until I met other people," Kyrah Simon, a senior at Marjory Stoneman Douglas High School who participated in the bus tour, said in an interview. "It's so crazy and surreal to see how what happened in my school inspired people all over the world."

CHAPTER 3

Opposition to and Criticism of Teen Activists

High school activists must balance their journey through adolescence with the weight of their commitments. With the fight for change comes opposition, both personal and political. The Parkland student activists in particular faced backlash and criticism from both their peers and politicians. Opposition has the power to discourage any activist, but today's teens face opposition with maturity and resolve.

The View From Opposite Sides of a Student Walkout in Montana

BY JULIE TURKEWITZ | MARCH 15, 2018

PLANS FOR THE student walkouts on Wednesday, when tens of thousands of people left their classrooms to protest gun violence, had stirred controversy for weeks in Montana, where the gun ownership rate outranks that in nearly every other state. In Billings, the state's most populous city, parents threatened to ground students who left their classrooms. And organizers of a walkout from Billings West High School changed a call for "gun reform" on their Facebook page to one for "school safety."

In the end, there were walkouts at three Billings high schools. At Billings West, administrators cleared the snow on the front lawn and hundreds of young people in a school of 1,800 came streaming out of their classrooms.

Two Billings West students share why they walked out — or stayed in class.

JARETH BROWN, 18

Favorite Class: Sociology
What he wants to be when he grows up: Actor, writer
Why he stayed in class: Jareth grew up with guns, and hunting is "a sacred thing" in his family.

He had seen coverage of mass shootings at other schools, and he initially considered participating in the walkout, to protest "the evil that is almost stirring within our country."

But as he watched the students organize over several weeks, he said, he realized that "some of the crowd would be walking out for the wrong reasons."

They wanted to skip class, he said. They wanted to "fraternize." And some students were calling for an outright ban on firearms like the AR-15.

Jareth is in favor of background checks. He said he was in favor of waiting periods for some weapons but not of a ban on the AR-15, since he thinks that would "infringe on the Second Amendment."

Jareth said that he realized his fellow students want to stop gun violence, but that he didn't think they had the right answers. He believed that his school needed to bring in another armed guard, and that it should allow teachers and students with proper licenses to bring firearms to school.

When the walkout began on Wednesday at 10 a.m., he sat in his English class as more than half of his classmates left.

"It was almost foolhardy," he said of the walkout. "To me it was a demonstration of a lot of our students here trying to represent that they believe they can make a change — but a lot of them don't know what that change is yet. To me they aren't quite ready and they don't know where to start."

BEN SHOLAR, 17
Favorite Class: Environmental science
What he wants to be when he grows up: Botanist
Why he walked out: The shooting in Parkland, Fla., left Ben heartbroken.

Another student approached him with the idea of the March 14 walk-out. A Facebook page went up, calling for "gun reform." Then the backlash began. Adults began harassing him on Facebook, he said. Students balled up protest fliers and threw them in his face. His group changed the protest's focus, he said, to "school safety."

Ben was not sure how many people would show up, but he walked out anyway. "I own a gun; my dad has a shotgun that I can use," he said. "But I just don't understand why we need military-grade weapons in our arsenal."

Hundreds of students gathered for the protest, he said. They joined hands and read the names of the Parkland victims.

"They don't know what they're talking about," he said of his critics, who were mostly adults. "Times have changed since they were in high school. We're a lot more politically active and involved in Montana than a lot of the people who grew up here."

Ben went on: "They don't have to grow up every day with the possibility of a person coming in with a gun. That's not on their mind. But it's on every high school student's mind."

MITCH SMITH contributed reporting from Chicago.

'Skinhead Lesbian' Tweet About Parkland Student Ends Maine Republican's Candidacy

BY MATT STEVENS | MARCH 18, 2018

A REPUBLICAN CANDIDATE for the Maine State House who disparaged two teenage survivors of the school shooting in Parkland, Fla., dropped out of the race after drawing heavy criticism and challengers from both political parties.

The candidate, Leslie Gibson, had been running to represent District 57 in central Maine unopposed, according to The Sun Journal, which first reported the comments he made on Twitter. Mr. Gibson called one Florida student, Emma González, a "skinhead lesbian," and another, David Hogg, a "moron" and a "baldfaced liar."

Some state lawmakers, including at least two Republicans, were quick to condemn Mr. Gibson after his comments surfaced. Mr. Hogg issued a call on Twitter for someone to run against Mr. Gibson. By Thursday, two challengers who had been dismayed by the remarks were scrambling to complete the paperwork needed to run for the seat before the filing deadline that night.

By Friday, at least one Democrat, Eryn Gilchrist, and one Republican, Thomas H. Martin Jr., had entered the race and Mr. Gibson had withdrawn.

Mr. Gibson could not be reached on Saturday and appeared to have deleted the personal Twitter account on which he made the remarks. But screenshots confirmed that a person with a Twitter handle bearing his name posted the disparaging tweets. Other screenshots of tweets from a locked account that appear to have been for Mr. Gibson's campaign contained an apology.

In the apologetic tweets, some of which were quoted by The Sun Journal, Mr. Gibson acknowledged that his responses were "harsh and uncivil" and said it was "inappropriate to single out" the students.

Mr. Martin, who served as a state senator in another district in 2011 and 2012 before losing a re-election bid, said he had considered running for office again but had not planned to do it so soon because he and his wife had just moved to the area and had adopted a baby boy.

Still, he said that after Mr. Gibson's comments, he got calls from friends urging him to run and decided that he "couldn't sit idle and let our state be reflected so negatively."

The comments "gave the state a black eye," Mr. Martin said.

"They weren't the true feelings of the state or the Republican Party — or any party — I have to believe," he said, adding that he planned to contact the Parkland students and commend their courage.

A spokesman for the Maine Republican Party did not return an email requesting comment on Saturday.

In a statement from the Maine Democratic Party, Ms. Gilchrist said she had not considered running for office before she read Mr. Gibson's comments. After she did, she said, she thought constituents in the district "deserved a representative who will respect people and try to work through their differences to make our lives better."

In the wake of the shooting last month at Marjory Stoneman Douglas High School, which killed 17 people, Ms. González, 18, and Mr. Hogg, 17, emerged as two of the most forceful student activists agitating for gun control.

Mr. Hogg's early remark that "we're children" while politicians "are the adults" won him praise. Ms. González's speech soon after made the phrase "We call B.S." a rallying cry among young people. Since then, the Parkland students' ability to leverage social media to command the narrative and keep gun control in the news has been widely recognized.

Ms. González did not return a phone message on Saturday night and did not appear to have responded to Mr. Gibson on Twitter directly. She did share a tweet from one of her fellow students who said Mr. Gibson's decision to drop out of the race was "what he deserves."

Mr. Hogg said his mother had seen a story about what Mr. Gibson had called Ms. González and he had quickly sent the tweet asking someone to challenge Mr. Gibson.

"If you're the type of person who calls children who are a witness to murder a skinhead lesbian and baldfaced liar, that kind of speaks for itself," he said on Saturday. "It's disgusting, but honestly, I'm a super petty person, and we all cheered when he said that he dropped out."

"We need good people in office — people who are actually human and have an ounce of empathy," he continued. "It's hilarious because its ridiculous. They're only proving our point that there are so many bad politicians out there. We almost let somebody that would say something like that win and run unopposed."

Why I Didn't Join My School's Walkout

OPINION | BY DAKOTA HANCHETT | MARCH 19, 2018

HANOVER, N.H. — I am a junior in high school, and I regularly shoot guns, for target practice and hunting. Going to school can be hard because most kids don't understand how I live. It can be uncomfortable to be a gun-owning teenager right now, when high schools have become the centers of gun control protests. But there are many of us around the country.

I own firearms not only because I think they are cool, but also because they are considered a tool in my family. I have been brought up around guns all my life. Yes, I have used AR-15 semiautomatic rifles, and old Civil War rifles, too. I live on a farm where I hunt wild game and butcher animals humanely. Some kids at my school don't understand why I hunt; they think that it is cruel and that raising beef cattle and chickens is bad. Sometimes I get the feeling these kids are afraid of me because I own firearms.

There was a walkout at my school last week. It was meant to honor the students who died in the school shooting in Florida, but it was also about protesting firearms. I didn't join in. I feel horrible about the kids who were killed or hurt, but firearms aren't the problem — people are.

I think people who use guns in mass shootings are using those guns to seek help. There are other ways to get help, but the people who do these things have probably asked for help or have shown signs that they need it but were let down by the adults around them.

Many of the young people protesting guns right now seem to have very little knowledge about gun rules and regulations. Guns can be used safely. My family and I talk frequently about firearms and how they should be used. I have a younger brother, and we teach him the rights and wrongs of firearm safety — and, of course, never to use guns to hurt people.

It's hard to talk about guns, as well as about hunting and farming, at school because no one there knows much about those three topics. They've been told not to touch or talk about guns, and some of the kids think it is just absolutely wrong for people to own them. That is their opinion, and I respect it and am open to talking about it. But even if people try to be nice, they don't really want to debate it.

At the school I used to go to, a few miles away across the border in Vermont, it was a totally different culture. There were a lot of parents and kids who owned and used guns, and pretty much everyone hunted. And it was a small town where everyone knew who you were.

Through the Hartford Area Career and Technology Center, I have met other friends who understand my family's culture. I study natural resources there for half of the school day, because I want to become a firefighter with a background in land management.

I believe in gun control and that there should be stricter rules that require all gun sellers to do federal background checks. I also think gun sellers have a responsibility to make their own decisions about whom they want to sell a gun to. If you buy a gun from a federally licensed seller, you have to do the federal background check, which can take more than an hour with all the paperwork. The gun seller should use common sense during that time to determine whether the buyer is in the right state of mind and will use a firearm only in legal ways.

Also, if we can teach students about sex and about drug and alcohol abuse, why can't we teach them about firearm safety? If we can be shown pictures of penises and vaginas, why can't we have a couple of police officers come in and show us an unloaded gun and talk about how to keep us safe?

That class would be for high school students, but if the school district thought it was working it could be spread to younger students. When I was 10, I took a hunter safety class through the New Hampshire Fish and Game Department at a nearby elementary school at night. It was free to everyone who was interested, and it was very safe because guns were not allowed to be loaded while on school property.

I think the people who are afraid of guns should talk to the people who are familiar with them, and both should keep an open mind. Even if people on the other side don't agree, they need to be respectful, listen, be honest and not get upset with the other person.

DAKOTA HANCHETT is a junior at Hanover High School.

Parkland Students Find Themselves Targets of Lies and Personal Attacks

BY JONAH ENGEL BROMWICH | MARCH 27, 2018

ONE WAS PHOTOSHOPPED tearing up the Constitution — a falsehood — and criticized for wearing a flag that represented her Cuban heritage.

A conservative blog said that another wasn't even at the school during the killings — then had to backtrack on Monday when that also proved false.

The attacks on the teenage survivors of the shooting in Parkland, Fla., have been fierce from the beginning, and have only continued since the students helped spearhead hundreds of protests this weekend.

Two of the most vocal survivors, Emma González, 18, and David Hogg, 17, have been targets of a disproportionate amount of vitriol.

In an interview Tuesday, Mr. Hogg said they had been singled out because of their prominence and emphasized that ad hominem attacks would not end school shootings.

"I mean, we're kind of the faces of the movement," he said. "Together we kind of form an unstoppable force that terrifies them."

He added that he and Ms. González were being attacked "because they know we're strong."

Here are a few of the recent attempts to discredit the students.

RedState, a conservative blog, questioned whether Mr. Hogg was even at the school on the day of the shooting, then backtracked Monday.

RedState, a conservative blog, ran an "update" Monday evening to a story it had published that questioned whether Mr. Hogg was present at Marjory Stoneman Douglas during the day of the shooting.

Emma González was criticized by a Republican congressman, Steve King, for wearing the Cuban flag on her jacket.

Sarah Rumpf, a writer for RedState, had questioned Mr. Hogg after watching an interview where he said he rode his bike to the school on the day of the shooting to interview his classmates.

The bike trip was described in a Vox article written in February. It indicated that Mr. Hogg had been at school during the shooting, as widely confirmed by many news organizations. He had left campus and then rode his bike back that evening to interview classmates.

Video has shown that Mr. Hogg was in a closet during the shooting. Ms. Rumpf eventually found the article and video, and apologized.

RedState struck through the old article, but did not describe the update as a correction, seeming to blame the misinformation on confusing reports elsewhere. The false report was spread by well-known conservatives, including Erick Erickson, who has contributed to The New York Times opinion section. Mr. Erickson later deleted his original tweet.

After his Facebook page posted an attack on Ms. González, Mr. King was criticized by some conservatives, including Frank Luntz.

A fake image of Ms. González tearing up the Constitution spread quickly over the weekend.

The doctored image of Ms. González ripping apart the Constitution of the United States, began to spread during the march on Saturday. It was falsified from a Teen Vogue image in which she was pictured ripping apart a paper shooting target.

The image, which exists in a gray area between meme and misinformation, was promoted on Gab, the alt-right alternative to Twitter, and by the right-wing actor Adam Baldwin.

Some claimed the image to be satire, and similar memes of President Trump and other political figures appear across the spectrum. But the political scientist Emily Thorson has pointed out that their spread contributes to a climate of misinformation, even if those who see the images understand them to be fake.

Ms. González was criticized for wearing a Cuban flag patch.

Steve King, the Republican congressman from Iowa, posted on Facebook about the Cuban flag sewn to Ms. González's jacket.

"This is how you look when you claim Cuban heritage yet don't speak Spanish," the post said, "and ignore the fact that your ancestors fled the island when the dictatorship turned Cuba into a prison camp, after removing all weapons from its citizens; hence their right to self-defense." It showed an image of her with the flag patch visible on her jacket.

The post and similar ones angered other survivors of gun violence and even some of Mr. King's fellow conservatives, who pointed out that the Cuban flag has long been used by dissidents from the Castro regime.

Ms. González retweeted Mr. Hogg's response to Mr. King: "She's a beautiful woman of Cuban descent and we love her. You would too if you ever got the chance to meet her."

She also retweeted another of Mr. Hogg's tweets, which called on Senator Marco Rubio, a Republican of Florida of Cuban descent, to respond to Mr. King.

Hey @marcorubio @Emma4Change s family fled Cuba to
escape totalitarianism and live in freedom just like your family could you please respond to @SteveKingIA

— David Hogg (@davidhogg111) Mar. 26, 2018

The conservative writer and commentator Dan McLaughlin suggested that reporters ask Ms. González "what the flag means to her and why she wears it." She did not respond to a call Tuesday.

The name-calling continues.

Many attacks on the Parkland students do not even pretend to focus on issues or substance. They include the false conspiracy trope that the students are paid actors. Sometimes their appearances and intelligence are mocked, including their efforts to get accepted to colleges this spring.

On Sunday, the conservative podcaster and vocal Trump supporter Bill Mitchell referred to Mr. Hogg as a "Damien, Children of the Corn, Hitler-Youth type" on Twitter.

The vitriol has sometimes backfired. A Republican candidate for the Maine State House dropped out of the race after calling Ms. González a "skinhead lesbian" and Mr. Hogg a "moron" and a "bald-faced liar."

In a Tuesday interview, Nicole Hockley, whose young son Dylan was killed in the 2012 school shooting in Newtown, Conn., advised the students to ignore the attacks as much as possible. She recalled that she had faced conspiracy theories and personal attacks after her 6-year-old son was killed along with 19 other first graders at Sandy Hook Elementary School.

She remembered how that felt: "All I'm trying to do is make it so this doesn't happen to other people and you're attacking me without a lot of basis."

She said that it was also important to hear rational criticism when trying to find common ground on the issues.

When dealing with more reasonable opponents and critics she tries to de-escalate the conversations, she said, to learn more about what they think and educate them about her views.

"Sometimes there's a new perspective that I haven't considered," she said, though she rarely finds such views persuasive. Still, she said, those conversations "can bear a lot of fruit."

Parkland Activist Got Some College Rejections. He'll Major in 'Changing the World.'

BY AUDRA D. S. BURCH | MARCH 29, 2018

MIAMI — Starting in the fall of 2017, David Hogg, a Marjory Stoneman Douglas High School senior, applied to a half-dozen universities that offered programs in journalism, political science or photography. His plan was to become a journalist or filmmaker.

Less than six months later, the Parkland, Fla., teenager had tragically become one of the best-known high school students in America. After 17 of his fellow students and teachers were killed in a Feb. 14 mass shooting, Mr. Hogg became a leader in the grass-roots, student-led gun control movement that spread around the country, pushing a campaign to hold lawmakers accountable for their votes on gun legislation.

The day after the shooting, Mr. Hogg got his first college application letter back: a rejection from California State University at Long Beach. At least two more denials followed, along with acceptances to three universities. Now Mr. Hogg, whose name and face are surely recognizable to college admissions officers everywhere, has no idea where or if he is going to college in the fall.

"Sure, it's disappointing and annoying, but not surprising. There are a lot of amazing people who do not get into or go to college," said Mr. Hogg, who carries a 4.2 GPA and scored 1270 on the SAT. "I wanted to make a difference through storytelling and political activism, but I am already doing that now."

The Parkland students are a case study in civic engagement. They are among the leaders of the #NeverAgain movement, collectively delivering fiery speeches that demand change, promoting their message on social media and organizing the March for Our

ERIN SCHAFF FOR THE NEW YORK TIMES

David Hogg, a Parkland student activist, raised his fist at the end of his speech at the March for Our Lives rally in Washington.

Lives rally held last weekend, which drew participants from across the globe.

Much of their leadership and community work, driven by the loss of classmates and friends, might not have been considered in the college admission process. Now, some of the most vocal Parkland seniors — whether accepted or denied to their top college choices — are rethinking their college plans, hoping in one way or another to capitalize on the momentum.

Samantha Fuentes, who was wounded by a bullet and shrapnel in the Parkland attack, is contemplating sitting out the first semester or even the full year to continue the campaign to promote more rigorous gun safety laws.

"If the movement is solidifying even more and hitting the nation from all directions and they need soldiers, I will put college off," said Ms. Fuentes, 18, who is staying close to home with tentative plans to attend Broward Community College, then Florida Atlantic University.

As a shooting victim and survivor, she is willing to speak at universities or to politicians about gun legislation.

"The truth is, us kids, we just want to be the voice for the people we lost, or for people who don't think they have a voice," said Ms. Fuentes, who would like to eventually become an elementary schoolteacher. "I am prioritizing this over college right now, I am prioritizing people's lives over my education."

University admissions offices declined to discuss individual applications, but many noted that civic engagement is a plus in considering whether to admit an applicant. In fact, some colleges publicly assured high school applicants in advance of last weekend's March for Our Lives rallies that their participation in peaceful protests would not harm admission chances.

Harvard, for example, issued a statement: "The mission of Harvard College is to provide a deeply transformative liberal arts and sciences education that will prepare our students for a life of citizenship and leadership. Fundamental to our mission is our belief that students have the right to protest peacefully about issues of concern to them. Students who are disciplined for engaging responsibly in exercising their rights and freedoms would not have their chances of admission compromised or their admissions revoked."

While on spring break this week, Mr. Hogg said he was leaning toward taking a gap year to focus on the midterm elections, hoping to rally young voters and target politicians supported by the National Rifle Association.

"We are trying to get these laws changed to drive down the number of people who die by gun violence," he said. "I can figure out everything else later."

Mr. Hogg said he does not believe his outspokenness had anything to do with the college denials, but admits it has been frustrating. In a late-night, March 16 message on Twitter — liked by at least 64,000 and retweeted nearly 6,600 times — Mr. Hogg told his followers, "Just got rejected from another college but that's ok we're already changing the world. Goodnight everyone."

He added that he was comforting himself by eating chocolate muffins. The response was mixed, with some mocking his rejection, some encouraging him to take a gap year and others touting him as precisely the type of student colleges should recruit.

After a Twitter follower suggested he apply to a California university, Mr. Hogg confirmed that one of the schools that denied his application was University of California, San Diego. The University of California, Los Angeles, also turned him down, he said later.

On Wednesday morning, Laura Ingraham, the conservative radio host, taunted Mr. Hogg by linking to a story on Twitter about his college application denials. "David Hogg Rejected by Four Colleges To Which He Applied and whines about it," she said. Mr. Hogg pushed back, calling for sponsors to boycott Ms. Ingraham's show. He later posted a list of advertisers to his nearly 600,000 followers, and Ms. Ingraham on Thursday apologized on Twitter.

"Any student should be proud of a 4.2 GPA," including Mr. Hogg, she wrote. "On reflection, in the spirit of Holy Week, I apologize for any upset or hurt my tweet caused him or any of the brave victims of Parkland."

Ryan Deitsch, a Parkland classmate who wants to follow his father and grandfather into filmmaking and photography, said his applications were rejected from several schools, including U.C.L.A. and Northwestern University. He was admitted to Florida State University, Savannah College of Art and Design and Columbia College Chicago.

"I don't know what the next couple of months will look like. Right now, we are ramped up and the world is watching so now is the time for us to act," Mr. Deitsch, 18, said just hours after a phone interview with Columbia College Hollywood, which is not affiliated with the Chicago school. "To do that, some of us might have to change our original plans. Right now, I am thinking of taking at least a semester off to devote to the movement."

Though the shooting and organized response thrust Parkland students into the spotlight, Mr. Deitsch, a student journalist who filmed students in the aftermath of the shooting, does not believe it entitles him to special college privileges.

"It's disappointing to not get into certain schools, but I try to keep things in perspective," he said. "I am not angry. If I didn't qualify then I shouldn't just be admitted because I spoke the loudest. There is much more important work for us to do."

'Almost No One Agrees With Us': For Rural Students, Gun Control Can Be a Lonely Cause

BY JACK HEALY | MAY 22, 2018

BENTON, KY. — The teenagers in rural Kentucky decided they were fed up after a 15-year-old with a handgun turned their high school into another killing ground, murdering two classmates. Like so many other students, they wrote speeches and op-ed essays calling for gun control, they painted posters and they marched on their State Capitol. The blush of activism made them feel empowered, even a little invincible.

Then came the backlash.

It started with sideways looks and laughter from other students in the hallways, they said. Friends deleted them from group chats and stopped inviting them over. On social media, people called the teenage activists "retards" and "spoiled brats," and said they should have been the ones to die during a shooting in Marshall County High School's student commons four months ago.

In a more liberal city like Parkland, Fla., or at a rally in Washington, these students might have been celebrated as young leaders. But in rural, conservative parts of the country where farm fields crackle with target practice and children grow up turkey hunting with their parents, the new wave of student activism clashes with bedrock support for gun rights.

Speaking out in a place like Marshall County, Ky., carries a price — measured in frayed friendships, arguments with parents and animosity within the same walls where classmates were gunned down.

The gulf between liberal and conservative America's responses to mass shootings was on display again in Santa Fe, Tex., population 13,000, after 10 people were killed at the high school there on Friday. Republican leaders expressed no desire to pass gun restrictions. Many

A billboard supporting the students of Marshall County High School in Benton, Ky. In January, two students at the school were killed in a shooting.

residents and students agreed with them, saying that gun control would not stop the bloodshed at America's schools.

"If we had more guns on campus with more teachers armed, we'd be a lot safer," said Layton Kelly, 17, a student who hid in a night-black classroom next to the scene of the shooting in Santa Fe.

That view resonates across rural Kentucky, where state lawmakers did not pass any new gun restrictions after the Marshall County shooting.

Most of the debate, both here in Benton, the hamlet that is home to the county high school, and at the State Capitol in Frankfort, has been focused on how to make schools more secure and how to detect potentially dangerous students. The school district in Marshall County has hired more armed officers and locked many of the high school's 86 doors. Every morning, teachers and staff members search students' backpacks and wand them with metal detectors.

A banner outside Personal Security Firearms, a gun shop in Benton.

"I don't think the Second Amendment is the issue," said Kevin Neal, Marshall County's judge/executive. "If somebody gets it in their head they're going to kill, they're going to do it."

Mr. Neal, a hulking former Marine, is a staunch gun rights supporter who said he carried a pistol on his side as he finished his lunch at JoJo's Café. He said that many adults thought the student protesters were simply "marching to march." Some parents said the students were being goaded by anti-gun groups outside Marshall County and were just seeking attention.

"They want to show, 'Look at me, look at me,' " said P. J. Thomason, whose son Case was wounded in the shooting. "Everyone that owns a gun is wrong — that's what they teach them nowadays."

Mr. Thomason said that Case survived that day because he is a competitive pistol and rifle shooter who recognized the sound of gunshots in the student commons and instantly knew to run. Case was struck in the hip, but recovered quickly and is shooting again.

Guns are popular in rural western Kentucky, where hunting and target shooting are common pastimes.

"The reason he's alive is because of a gun," Mr. Thomason said.

The Marshall County students who decided to speak out for gun control said they understood the consequences of bucking the views of many of their parents, friends and neighbors on an issue as personal and emotional as guns.

"We knew we were going to get backlash," said Cloi Henke, 15, who was in a small group of students who participated in a local March for Our Lives rally one rainy day this spring.

"I just didn't think it would be so forward," said her 15-year-old friend Lily Dunn. "When people started talking about me, it knocked me down a few pegs."

It was just after school one afternoon, and Cloi, Lily and their friends — all freshmen — were squeezed into a booth at the Benton Dairy Queen. Since the shooting at Marshall, they cocoon together often, in their spot in the student commons or on a friend's willow-

From left, Hailey Case, Jordan Harrell and Lily Dunn at Jordan's home in Calvert City, Ky. The three, freshmen at Marshall County High, have been active in calling for gun restrictions since the shooting at their school.

shaded back porch, to support each other and strategize about their tiny slice of the gun control movement.

"Almost no one agrees with us," said Hailey Case, 16. That includes her father, who argued with Hailey after listening to her practice a speech she delivered at the local March for Our Lives rally.

One girl threatened to fight them after they held a gun control rally, they said. Letters and commenters in local news media said the students were too young to know anything.

Cloi said she had been at a friend's house one afternoon when her friend's father pulled out his AR-15 to show her "what you guys are trying to ban."

"It was kind of scary," Cloi said.

Lily, sitting next to her, said a teacher had confronted her when she came to class wearing a T-shirt in the school's orange and blue colors,

ANDREA MORALES FOR THE NEW YORK TIMES

A shop window displayed a sign of solidarity with the high school.

showing a constellation of dots for every school in Kentucky that had been affected by a shooting.

Their own dot came on Jan. 23. According to the police and prosecutors, Gabriel Parker, a 15-year-old student at Marshall County High, opened fire on a group of students with his stepfather's handgun as a kind of twisted social experiment, to see how people would react. Mr. Parker was arrested after he slipped out of the school among a group of students fleeing the carnage, and has been charged as an adult in the attack.

Across the country, about 60 percent of rural households own a gun — double the rate of city households — and many Marshall County students said that before the shooting they had barely thought about the gun debate. They hunted and shot air rifles at camp on Kentucky Lake, and their fathers kept handguns for protection.

Afterward, though, the gulf between their views and their parents' became impossible to ignore.

A bouquet of flowers left at the entrance to the school in memory of the students who were killed.

Mary Cox, 18, a senior who is involved in theater and captain of her Speech team, got into arguments with her father when he tried to buy her a compact handgun to take with her to college. One day, she said, when her father was driving her home from a rehearsal, he pressed her on her support for banning AR-15s. If she was being attacked, wouldn't she want someone with an AR-15 to come help?

"We couldn't be more opposite in what we believe," her father, Ezra, said in an interview. Still, he said, he and his wife had encouraged Mary to stay true to her beliefs.

One evening, three freshman friends who spoke at a gun control rally drove through town on their way to dinner, gliding past "Marshall Strong" signs on the Arby's and the Lake Chem Credit Union. Four months after the shooting, reminders linger everywhere. Blue-and-orange lawn signs poke up from drainage ditches. Bible verses

Hailey in an "Enough Is Enough" T-shirt.

about faith and healing are still painted onto the windows of antique shops and insurance agencies downtown.

"I don't want to see it any more," Lela Free said, staring out from a back seat.

Sitting in front in the passenger seat, Korbin Brandon, 16, thought about how his life had changed since 7:55 a.m. on that day in January.

Korbin, a freshman who speaks like a cross between Encyclopedia Brown and Alex Keaton, the conservative teenager from "Family Ties," had always thought of himself as a Second Amendment supporter and a sportsman. He'd fired a high-powered rifle when he was 8 years old.

But on Jan. 23, he was turned to face the glass walls that overlook the student commons when his classmates were being cut down.

"I saw some stuff" is how he puts it.

Though he still calls himself a conservative, Korbin decided to join the students who were organizing speeches and rallies focused on safety and gun control. When he returned to class after giving a speech that confronted the National Rifle Association, one friend yelled at him; others took a group photo without him; and a deacon at his church warned him that he sounded like a Democrat.

"They said I'd betrayed them," Korbin said of his friends. "I'd turned my back on the good way, the sportsman's way. I faced a lot of ridicule."

He was surprised at the backlash, because he does not support banning guns or accessories. But he said they should perhaps be harder to buy.

He has since tried to patch up those strained relationships, and quoted a Bible verse about avoiding foolish controversies to rebut one person who criticized him. He shrugged off the effects on him. So many other people in his hometown had suffered deeply from that terrible January day.

"There's other people that need to be taken care of," he said.

'Swatting' Prank Sends Police to Home of David Hogg, Parkland Survivor

BY DANIEL VICTOR AND MATTHEW HAAG | JUNE 5, 2018

AN UNKNOWN CALLER falsely reported on Tuesday that there was someone with a weapon inside the home of David Hogg, a survivor of the February shooting at Marjory Stoneman Douglas High School in Parkland, Fla., who has become a prominent gun-control advocate.

The 911 call, which came in at 8:29 a.m., caused SWAT teams and officers in tactical gear to respond to the recent graduate's home, according to the Broward County Sheriff's Office.

A potentially dangerous situation was averted when officers determined no one was home; Mr. Hogg, 18, and his mother were in Washington to accept a human rights award. "I think it's really a distraction from what we're trying to fix here, which is the massive gun violence epidemic in this country," Mr. Hogg told Local 10 News in Miami.

Such hoax calls — known as swatting — are typically intended to force armed officers to converge upon an unsuspecting target's home, creating a spectacle and, at best, a terrifying inconvenience for all involved.

At worst, they can be deadly.

In December, two men, Casey Viner and Shane Gaskill, got in an argument while playing an online video game, and Mr. Viner enlisted Tyler Barriss to swat Mr. Gaskill, according to a grand jury indictment. Mr. Gaskill, egging them on, provided a false address for his home.

Mr. Barriss called the police in Wichita, Kan., telling them that he had killed his father, was holding two family members at gunpoint, had doused his house in gasoline and was contemplating suicide. The police arrived at the address they were given, and a police officer fatally shot Andrew Finch, 28, in his doorway after he stepped outside to investigate the commotion.

An officer said Mr. Finch had not complied when instructed to put his hands up and made a gun-drawing motion, according to The Wichita Eagle.

Mr. Viner, Mr. Gaskill and Mr. Barriss are facing federal charges; Mr. Barriss is also facing involuntary manslaughter charges in state court. The police officer has not been charged.

A Broward County Sheriff's Office spokeswoman said responding officers were aware that the address they were given on Tuesday was Mr. Hogg's home, but did not say whether they had responded to previous "swatting" calls there.

Mr. Hogg has become one of the most outspoken gun-control advocates to emerge out of the shooting in Parkland, where 17 of his fellow students and teachers were killed on Feb. 14. In the immediate aftermath of the shooting, he began gaining international plaudits and legions of social media followers for his anti-gun commentary, unafraid to directly target politicians and policies he saw as destructive.

That same commentary has made him an enemy of gun-rights defenders, and he has endured name-calling, personal attacks and outright lies, including a trending video that falsely claimed he was a crisis actor.

Laura Ingraham, a Fox News host, taunted him in March for being rejected from colleges, leading to several companies pulling advertising from her show. Jamie Allman, a conservative commentator in the St. Louis area, lost his TV and radio jobs after threatening Mr. Hogg in a tweet.

Mr. Hogg graduated on Sunday in a ceremony that honored four seniors who were killed in February. He was in Washington on Tuesday to accept the Robert F. Kennedy Human Rights award for March for Our Lives, the nonprofit organization he and other students created after the shooting.

Senator Bill Nelson, a Democrat from Florida, spoke to Mr. Hogg about the swatting episode on Tuesday, according to The Miami Herald.

"These students are getting all kinds of threats and it's going beyond threats, they're getting actual incidents," Mr. Nelson told the newspaper. "And it's a shame that we can't have a discourse in America over the issue of gun safety that people have to take it out in a way of attempted intimidation of these students."

'Let Us Have a Childhood': On the Road With the Parkland Activists

BY MAGGIE ASTOR | AUG. 15, 2018

They're registering voters. They're spotlighting the work of local organizers. They're talking about all forms of gun violence.

SIX MONTHS AND A DAY after a gunman massacred 17 of their classmates and staff, the students of Marjory Stoneman Douglas High School woke up Wednesday and began a new year.

For the past two months, a busload of them have traveled the country in pursuit of stricter gun laws, connecting with local activists, holding rallies, debating counterprotesters and, above all, registering voters.

They knew perfectly well how many before them — after Columbine, after Sandy Hook, after Orlando — had been unable to turn outrage into lasting change. But this time was different. Since the shooting, state legislatures have passed at least 50 gun regulations, largely because of public pressure created by the Parkland movement. So The New York Times spent three days on the road with the March for Our Lives activists to find out what changed.

AUG. 1: GREENSBORO, N.C.
It's not about banning guns

They started the day where the sit-ins began nearly 60 years ago, at a Woolworth's lunch counter pristinely preserved within the International Civil Rights Center and Museum.

Remember, said the museum's chief executive, John L. Swaine, the movement that would desegregate lunch counters across the South started with just four people — and they were your age.

From the sunny lobby, the students descended into the galleries. They saw the lunch counter. They saw a brick archway engraved with the words "COLORED ENTRANCE." They saw an image of Emmett Till's mutilated body.

Only "in the halls of Congress," had she ever felt as helpless as she did on her classroom floor on Feb. 14, said Lauren Hogg, 15.

At the end, they saw a wall covered in a mosaic of civil rights activists' faces. Here and there were blank spaces. "We left them open for you," said their tour guide, Dillon Tyler.

It was, he said, his "true honor" to give them this tour — because 12 years ago, it was his school that was shot up.

Mr. Tyler, now 26, was a freshman at Orange High School in Hillsborough, N.C., when a gunman came in 2006. Though no one was killed there, "we were trapped in that school for five hours," he said, his voice breaking. "Meanwhile, all you heard was bullets and screams."

The room was silent as he finished speaking. Then Sara Jado, 18, a member of March for Our Lives Greensboro, emerged from the crowd and hugged him. For more than 10 seconds, she did not let go.

As Ms. Jado retreated, Emma González, 18, stepped forward. Then another student. And another. They didn't speak. They just opened their arms, and Mr. Tyler cried on their shoulders.

Emma González, a Parkland student, and Dillon Tyler, who survived a school shooting in North Carolina 12 years ago.

These are the bonds that linked everyone on this tour: trauma, and fear, and the knowledge that any of them could be next. Some fell asleep to the sound of gunfire as children in Chicago or Milwaukee. Now they were meeting with people who bore the scars of mass shootings more than a decade old. And they were joined by 15-year-olds who spoke casually about which classrooms had good escape routes, and which ones they were likely to die in.

"Let us have a childhood," Anne Joy Cahill-Swenson, a rising sophomore at Grimsley High School in Greensboro, told the crowd at LeBauer Park that evening. "This is not something we should have to worry about."

Across the street, a dozen or so counterprotesters with red MAGA caps, "I Plead the 2nd" posters and a QAnon sign were on the sidewalk, shouting at Matt Deitsch, a 2016 graduate of Stoneman Douglas and the chief strategist for March for Our Lives.

Ramon Contreras and Matt Deitsch spoke with Jason Passmore, a counterprotester.

"Violence will happen if people try to take guns away from us," warned one of them, Jason Passmore, 33.

Mr. Deitsch, 20, has a seemingly endless supply of statistics, and he chooses his words carefully. "People define 'assault weapon' in entirely different ways," he said later. "People define 'gun control' in completely different ways. And for the most part, we've tried to back away from using those terms."

Sometimes this works. Ramon Contreras, 19, who founded Youth Over Guns after a friend was killed, recalled that at a tour stop in Texas, he and a counterprotester came "this close" to agreeing on the need for safe storage of firearms. They exchanged contact information and still talk.

Other times, it doesn't work.

"I love this country," Mr. Deitsch told the protesters in North Carolina at one point.

"Do you?" Nancy Browning said doubtfully.

Nancy Browning and other counterprotesters in Greensboro.

But an interesting thing happens when you start talking. It turns out Ms. Browning, 45, supports closing a gun show loophole and banning bump stocks. And universal background checks? "Absolutely!" she said. "I don't think anybody should just be able to go get a gun."

"I just don't want them to come in and just want to completely blame guns for everything," she added. "The gun is not the problem."

Here lies the disconnect: the chasm between the policies March for Our Lives promotes and the policies many opponents think it promotes. The students don't want to abolish gun ownership. Some of their families own guns.

There is also an irony to the objection that they "blame guns for everything." They don't. At every stop, they emphasize that gun violence can't be addressed without addressing what fuels it: racism, poverty, substandard schools and mental health services. They speak daily about intersectionality, systems of oppression, the school-to-prison pipeline.

The students, including Ms. González, Mr. Contreras and David Hogg, unwound at a restaurant.

In fact, they talk about these things so much that it's easy to forget they are, well, teenagers. People who hold an impromptu dance party outside a theater when one of them starts banging out the "Pirates of the Caribbean" theme on a bright green piano. People who talk about prom and mock each other's pool shots and stuff cupcakes into their mouths whole.

AUG. 2: BLACKSBURG, VA.
The movement is bigger than Parkland

Half an hour before the students' panel on Thursday, the line outside the Lyric Theater stretched so far that people in the back fretted they would be turned away.

Inside, the eight panelists assembled. Only two, Ryan Deitsch and Lauren Hogg, were Parkland students. The others were Mr. Contreras, from New York; Tallulah Costa and Louis Garcia, high schoolers

Geoffrey Preudhomme, 23, and Ms. Hogg before a panel in Blacksburg.

in Roanoke, Va.; Matt Post, a recent high school graduate from Maryland; Geoffrey Preudhomme, of the Radford University Young Democrats; and Ryan Wesdock, of the Virginia Green Party.

It was as good an illustration as any of how the Parkland students wanted to organize the movement. They were adamant that it was not *their* movement. They understood that they wouldn't have such a platform if their town were not wealthy and mostly white — the sort of place where senseless violence is not "supposed" to happen.

"When we did the Peace March on the South Side of Chicago, they've been doing that for years — but all of a sudden, now that we showed up there, there were 10,000 people instead of 500," said David Hogg, 18. Last month, he added, he and the other students met a teenager in Oakland, Calif., who had lost 20 friends to gun violence, but Americans don't know their names.

This dynamic can be demoralizing for the people working without recognition. Bria Smith, 17, from Milwaukee, said she had spent a year

Colin Goddard, a survivor of the Virginia Tech shooting, led the group to a memorial.

working with local nonprofits and Black Lives Matter, but felt no one was listening. "Why would I do so much work and give so much energy of myself to a city that doesn't care if I'm doing it in the first place?" she asked.

Then she spoke at the March for Our Lives rally in Milwaukee, which led to a seat on a panel when the bus tour went there. Afterward, she recalled, an organizer asked if she wanted to join for more stops. (Her reply: "Give me a second. I have to call my mom and ask her first.")

Ms. Smith used to see Milwaukee as a prison to escape. But now, "I've met so many different youth who had wanted to make a difference in their communities, but never knew how to use their voice and their platform to do that," she said. "So after Road to Change, I'm going to come back, and I'm going to go to Milwaukee, and I'm going to be that voice for all the people who felt hopeless."

This is the biggest change of all. The students defined the problem itself differently, as gun violence writ large: not just mass shootings

Mr. Preudhomme, Ryan Wesdock and Bria Smith before the Blacksburg panel.

but gang killings, police brutality, domestic abuse, suicide. They talked about sharing their platform and using it to "raise the voices" of the activists who have been organizing in obscurity — several of whom, like Ms. Smith and Mr. Contreras, joined the tour. They tried to build infrastructure everywhere they went, coordinating with local people who would continue the work when the bus was gone.

Above all, they urged young people to vote. Many of their proposals already have widespread support. It's Congress and state legislatures, they say, that don't reflect the will of the people.

AUG. 3: CHARLOTTESVILLE, VA.
'Every single person that has died, I do it for them'

By 6 p.m. on Friday, Ms. González was lying on the floor of a back room at the Westminster Presbyterian Church, answering questions with her eyes closed.

Susan Bro, whose daughter was killed in Charlottesville, urged the students to pace themselves.

She was getting a cold. Mr. Hogg, cross-legged next to her, was getting over one. At least two other students were sick, too. None of them were getting enough sleep.

Earlier, the students had met with Susan Bro, whose daughter, Heather Heyer, was killed here a year ago this week when a white supremacist drove into a crowd.

"Some of you may have experienced this — it's hard to get out of bed, because I can get weighed down in the grief," Ms. Bro, 61, told them. "And then I'm like, 'No, there's work to do.' "

The work is grueling. Jaclyn Corin, 17, contacted every local organizer before every event, and spent every day "going to events while organizing future events at the same time." Before the shooting, she had 100 contacts in her phone. Now, she has over 600.

"My texts never stop coming in," she said. "I will wake up at 2 o'clock in the morning in the middle of the night to get a drink of water,

Buttons featuring an early rallying cry of the Parkland students were sold at the events.

and I'll answer my five texts that I missed in those two hours that I was sleeping."

She and the rest of the students run the show. The handful of adults with them were there mainly to handle things that minors can't, like booking hotel rooms.

"We entirely control everything we do," Mr. Hogg said. "Anybody above 20 on the bus works for us."

This is exhausting. It's also empowering.

"I just remember being in those days and not immediately thinking I needed my parents' help," Ms. González said to Ms. Bro, recalling the week after the shooting. "It just was not our first instinct to get help from anybody except for ourselves."

Then, the students were galvanized by the friends they had just lost, and they were desperate to prevent more massacres. Six months later, they have a vastly broader view of the problems they want to fix, and a vastly longer list of people to fix them for.

Ms. Hogg on a shuttle bus in Charlottesville. Six months after the shooting, the students have a broader view of the problems they want to fix.

Ms. Corin leapt in the day after the shooting because she had been on a dance team with one of the victims, Jaime Guttenberg. But now, she said, when she struggles to keep up the pace, she thinks of Philando Castile, too, and Michael Brown. She thinks of the young woman in Oakland who lost so many friends.

"This movement was started because of those 17, but it's become so much more than that," Ms. Corin said. "Every single place we go, I take those people's stories, their stories of loss and pain, and I carry them with me. And every single person that has died, I do it for them now."

What Three Days With the Parkland Student Activists Taught Me

TIMES INSIDER | BY MAGGIE ASTOR | AUG. 16, 2018

Times Insider delivers behind-the-scenes insights into how news, features and opinion come together at The New York Times.

SOMETIME AROUND 8 P.M., in the loft of a pub in downtown Greensboro, N.C., Emma González sank the 13 ball in a corner pocket, yelled in triumph and did a little dance.

As I jotted these details down, David Hogg came around the pool table with his cue, glanced at my notebook and gave me a strange look. I was keeping score?

I wasn't. But I really wanted to capture these students — the activists of Parkland, Fla., high schoolers who have become what Ms. González and Mr. Hogg later described, resignedly, as "international celebrities" — as the ordinary people they are. This gets lost, because the work they're doing isn't ordinary: This summer, they set out on a national tour to register voters and organize in pursuit of stricter gun legislation. But they're still teenagers, too young even to drink in the pub where they were playing, and they trash-talk each other over bad pool shots and do victory dances over good ones.

It's been six months since a former student opened fire in their high school and killed 17 students and staff members. In the aftermath, these students became instant activists. I spent three days this month with them and the young advocates they'd picked up along the way.

I learned, as I wrote in my article, just how much work went into planning the tour: The lead organizer, 17-year-old Jaclyn Corin, will sleep for two hours and then wake up to answer more texts. I learned how much they are emphasizing the broad scope of gun violence, a problem that goes far beyond mass shootings in suburban high schools. I talked to people like Bria Smith of Milwaukee, who used to

The 18-year-old activist Emma González plays pool after a day of appearances in Greensboro, N.C.

feel she had "no voice," and Ramon Contreras of New York, who used to be frustrated by how much attention the Parkland students were getting when activists like him had been working for years. They both talked about how inclusive the movement was, and how that gave them hope.

These points are crucial in explaining how this movement is different from all the ones that didn't work. But there were other things I was determined to capture, too. I wanted to capture the students' youth, and their humanity. ("A lot of our innocence was taken away from us, but our youth wasn't," Lauren Hogg, David's younger sister, mused in one group discussion. "I think that's a really powerful thing.") And I wanted to capture what it was like behind the scenes of this movement — the messy, stressful work that goes into creating something that appears so polished.

To do that, I had to talk to the students. But more important, I had to see them.

So I introduced myself — and then, for much of the first two days, I stood back and watched. As a tour guide led us through the galleries of the International Civil Rights Center and Museum in Greensboro, the students' media handler came over to me and whispered that he could pull aside anyone I wanted to interview. I said no thanks. I had three days to interview the students. I didn't want to interrupt an event to do it.

I still got the interviews I needed before I went home. But in the meantime, I was able to take in the museum's exhibits just as the students were. I was able to note their body language and their expressions. And then, when I thought the tour was over, the guide, Dillon Tyler, revealed that he had also survived a school shooting.

I was watching quietly when he got choked up. I was watching quietly when four people emerged from the crowd, one after another, to hug him as he cried. It was the most powerful moment of my three days on the tour. The room was silent. I was trying not to cry myself.

The students are strong by necessity. Their public face is that of, for example, Ms. Hogg, who was animated and confident at a panel in Blacksburg, Va. But afterward, she was subdued. At one point, out on the sidewalk, she was crying. These are the moments that remind you that she is 15 and lost four friends only half a year ago.

My main challenge was this: I was committed to respecting their need for time on their own, with the cameras off. But I also wanted to see how they interacted when the cameras were off. I didn't want to add to their emotional burdens, but I wanted to understand them. I didn't want to present them as superheroes. They're not. They're grieving, and they're tired. They're just still going.

CHAPTER 4

Where Do We Go From Here?

Teen activists have more resources in the 21st century than ever before. They have the world at their fingertips through social media. They have access to information and platforms on which to make their voices heard. Institutions like schools, universities and courts are starting to listen. What can be learned from teen activists in the global community? How will organized movements continue to change with the involvement of young activists? Teenagers will not be teenagers forever. What does the future hold for a growing generation of change-makers?

Malala Yousafzai, Youngest Nobel Peace Prize Winner, Adds to Her Achievements and Expectations

BY JODI KANTOR | OCT. 10, 2014

THOUGH MALALA YOUSAFZAI is 17, she does not use Facebook or even a mobile phone lest she lose focus on her studies. She spent her summer vacation flying to Nigeria to campaign for the release of girls kidnapped by the extremist Islamist group Boko Haram, but also worrying about her grades, which recently took a worrisome dip. She confronted President Obama about American drone policy in a meeting last year, but finds it difficult to befriend her fellow students in Birmingham, England.

Malala Yousafzai at the United Nations last year. Ms. Yousafzai, 17, is the youngest recipient of the Nobel Peace Prize.

"I want to have fun, but I don't quite know how," she wrote in the edition of her autobiography for young readers.

On Friday, Ms. Yousafzai became the youngest winner of the Nobel Peace Prize — grouped in the same pantheon as the Rev. Dr. Martin Luther King Jr. and Mother Teresa, and yet still a student at Edgbaston High School for Girls, where she was summoned out of her chemistry class to hear the news.

Ms. Yousafzai began campaigning for girls' education at the age of 11, three years before she was shot by the Taliban. She was so young that some observers questioned how well equipped a child of that age could be to put her own safety on the line and commit to a life of activism. The prize she received on Friday validates what she has taken on, but also underscores the disproportionate expectations that trail her: Can she truly influence the culture of her home country of Pakistan, which she cannot even visit because of threats to her safety, and where many revile her as a tool of the West? Ms. Yousafzai may be an Anne Frank-like figure who defied terror, showed extraordinary courage and inspires hope, but how much can one teenager accomplish?

"Can she actually create systemic change at this young age? Can she create a movement? Because she doesn't have that kind of infrastructure in Pakistan at the moment," said Vishakha Desai, a professor of international relations at Columbia, said in a telephone interview.

In one half of Ms. Yousafzai's dual life, she is the center of an international advocacy operation for girls' education that now involves a nonprofit organization, two best-selling books, and activities that stretch from Pakistan to Jordan to Kenya. She criticizes not just the Taliban, but also the culture of Pakistan, in which women are rarely granted the same rights and opportunities as men. She has become one of the world's most prominent faces of moderate Islam, saying in a recent interview that she tried wearing a burqa when she was younger but gave it up: "I realized that it just took away my freedom, and that's why I stopped wearing it."

When she met with Mr. Obama last year, she critiqued American military action in her home region. "Instead of soldiers, send books. Instead of sending weapons, send pens," as she later put it. (Asked how he responded, she gave a knowing look. "He's a politician," she said.)

In the other, lesser-known half of Ms. Yousafzai's life, she lives in a neat brick house near the hospital in Birmingham where she convalesced after being shot by the Taliban in 2012. She has largely recovered, but in her memoir and a recent interview, she spoke of longing for home and straining to fit in to her new environs. She spends hours on Skype each week with a childhood friend in Pakistan, catching up on girls' education efforts in the Swat Valley but also hometown gossip.

When she first moved to England, she found the clothing on other women so skimpy that she wondered if there was a national fabric shortage. She wears a standard British uniform to school each day — green sweater, striped shirt, tights — but adds a longer skirt and a headscarf for modesty. She still goes to therapy sessions to regain the use of her facial muscles, she wrote in her book, and tries not to dwell on the operations she may need in the future. She has grown to love cupcakes, but does not hide the fact that she and her family find England cold and isolating.

"We are just a few feet away from the next house, but for all we know of our neighbor it might as well be a mile," she wrote of her new life.

"It's odd to be so well known but to be lonely at the same time," she added.

And yet in an interview last August, Ms. Yousafzai exuded an almost ascetic sense of higher purpose, saying that she rarely watches television and deleted the Candy Crush game from her iPad to forestall a growing addiction. She allows herself to take selfies, she said, but only if they are employed for higher purposes: "We have to use it to highlight the issues that children all over the world are facing, so to highlight the issues girls are facing in Afghanistan or Pakistan or India," she said. As a child in Pakistan, she had access to only a handful of books, she said, but one was a biography of Dr. King, giving her an early sense of what one activist could accomplish.

Albert Schweitzer won the Nobel Peace Prize after a lifetime of medical and humanitarian work, and Aung Sang Suu Kyi won it after decades of human rights protest in Myanmar, but Ms. Yousafzai is so young that her future path still seems unclear. She often says that she wants to become a leader in Pakistan like another of her heroes, Benazir Bhutto, the first female prime minister of Pakistan, assassinated in 2007. That aspiration gives chills to Ms. Yousafzai's admirers, who worry about her continued safety.

Ever the education crusader, Ms. Yousafzai says she is focused on attending university. She would like to study at Oxford, followed perhaps by graduate school in the United States.

In a brief speech in Birmingham on Friday, she called the prize "an encouragement for me to go forward and believe in myself."

She added one stipulation, though: "It's not going to help me in my tests and exams."

Malala Yousafzai, Girls' Education Advocate, Finishes High School

BY DANIEL VICTOR | JULY 7, 2017

IT'S NOT UNUSUAL for teenagers to take a summer trip after graduating high school, but Malala Yousafzai is a bit different.

The 19-year-old Pakistani woman attended her last day of secondary school in Birmingham, England, on Friday, a milestone for the activist who has fought for girls' education. She said on her new Twitter account that she would begin traveling next week to the Middle East, Africa and Latin America to meet with girls.

"I enjoyed my school years, and I am excited for my future," she wrote in her blog. "But I can't help thinking of millions of girls around the world who won't complete their education."

Ms. Yousafzai became the youngest winner of the Nobel Peace Prize in 2014, having risen to international prominence as a voice against Islamist violence. She escaped to Britain in 2012 after being shot in the head by the Taliban when she was 15.

She founded the Malala Fund in 2013, an advocacy organization to ensure girls' education worldwide. In April, she visited Lancaster, Pa., and Ottawa, Canada, as the first two stops on her world tour.

She plans to attend college but has not said where. In an interview with Teen Vogue in April, she said she was as nervous about college as any other recent graduate.

"It is quite a good moment because you live without your parents and you live in a college, and that's the exciting part," she said. "After that I'm not sure what I'm going to do in terms of career, but I'm really sure that I'm going to be focused on the Malala Fund and the work we do for girls' education, so that's going to be my mission."

'Where My Activists At?' Inside the First Teen Vogue Summit

BY SHEILA MARIKAR | DEC. 5, 2017

LOS ANGELES — Around 9 a.m. on Saturday, a long line of artfully clad young women was forming around a beige corporate park. They had flown, driven, pleaded with their parents and assembled posses for the inaugural Teen Vogue Summit: a two-day event, costing from $299-$549 per ticket.

"This has been a dream come true," said Karishma Bhuiyan, 18, surveying her peers walking down a boardwalk lined with socially conscious vendors, a sort of "woke" mall. "I didn't think it was going to be this diverse. I'm shook. Like, wow, I do not want to go back to Dallas."

Under its editor Elaine Welteroth and digital editorial director Phillip Picardi, Teen Vogue added the political issues of today to coverage of party frocks and makeup tips, and became a glossy guidebook for readers disenfranchised by the current presidential administration. The summit was organized to inspire, educate — and yes, sell to — the young readers of what ceased to be a traditional magazine in November, when Condé Nast announced it would stop printing it regularly.

"Doing events has always been part of our heritage, thinking about these events in increasingly ambitious ways is new," said Josh Stinchcomb, Condé Nast's chief experience officer. "We're seeing huge interest among consumers and marketers for experiential activations."

Ms. Bhuiyan initially applied for one of 50 scholarships for this particular experiential activation, which was attended by 650 people on Saturday. When she didn't get accepted, she and her friend, Muram Ibrahim, 17, started a GoFundMe campaign. They raised over $2,900.

Over the weekend, more than 500 people attended the Teen Vogue Summit: a two-day event, costing from $299-$549 per ticket.

Still, "it took a lot of convincing of my mom to let me go," Ms. Ibrahim said.

"I made a Google presentation for my parents and I presented for one hour," Ms. Bhuiyan said.

Ava Liversidge, 13, started reading Teen Vogue because she aspires to work in fashion — she wore an Ikea T-shirt procured from a vintage store the previous day — but said it had opened her up to politics. "It encourages you to be interested in other things," she said. "It's a great, great resource."

A vast lawn was covered with folding chairs and furry beanbag loungers. Chloe x Halle, an R&B duo, sang a song and commanded the crowd to chant affirmations: "I am unstoppable," "I am funny."

Ms. Welteroth, in a blush-colored dress, ascended the stage to a hero's welcome. "Where my activists at?" she called, inciting cheers.

Muram Ibrahim, 17, and Karishma Bhuiyan, 18, started a GoFundMe campaign in order to attend the summit.

A keynote speaker was Hillary Clinton, interviewed by Yara Sha-hidi, a 17-year-old actress best known for her role on the sitcom "black-ish." Ms. Clinton urged her audience to combat mansplaining ("Be willing to say, 'I'm so glad John agrees with my idea'") and adjust their expectations at the polls ("Don't look for the perfect campaign and the perfect candidate").

Attendees broke into smaller groups for workshops, "mentor sessions" and panels. Cindy Gallop, a British advertising consultant, told one of these smaller audiences that "we need to build our own financial ecosystem because the white male one isn't working for us," and suggested that would-be employees walk into salary negotiations with "a number in your mind so large, you almost want to laugh when you say it."

Those who bought tickets for Friday's program were also able to meet female bosses at the Los Angeles offices of Instagram, YouTube, Netflix and other companies.

KENDRICK BRINSON FOR THE NEW YORK TIMES

Hillary Clinton was the keynote speaker at the summit. The actress Yara Shahidi interviewed her.

Hot merchandise included a $39 crop top that read "resist the gaslight." Juicy Couture bedazzled velour track jackets (for Generation Z, everything '90s is new again).

On the lawn, Autumn De Forest, 16, an artist and a member of Teen Vogue's 21 Under 21 list — the bar of public achievement getting so low one might limbo under it — bopped around with a new friend, Em Odesser, 17, the editor in chief of Teen Eye magazine (published quarterly). "This is the first time I've been in a teen-centric, girl-centric space," said Ms. Odesser, who lives in a suburb of New York. "Our school, it's very different from anything like this. I think safe spaces get a really bad rep. People see it as, 'Aw, these liberal, triggered snowflakes,' but to have a place where you can convene and create great things with each other is really, really important."

Of Ms. Welteroth, Ms. Odesser said, "She's the dream editor, and I'm so excited to hopefully meet her and compliment her on her white boots."

The actresses Storm Reid, center, and Rowan Blanchard, right, engaged their fans at the summit.

Back on the lawn, a panel called "How to Be a Better Ally" was wrapping up. The sun was setting, and some girls had wrapped themselves in blankets. "Now is not the time to get tired," commanded a hype man by the stage. "We are as woke as we were this morning, we are more woke than we were this morning." There remained discussions, mentor sessions, workshops. Maxine Waters, the California congresswoman, would be on soon. There would be ice cream before her, and a poetry performance afterward.

"Old Karishma is not here anymore," said Ms. Bhuiyan, springing up from a beanbag. "I'm totally new and improved. I want to go out and change the world right now, but, like, the event is still going on."

How the Parkland Students Got So Good at Social Media

BY JONAH ENGEL BROMWICH | MARCH 7, 2018

THE SECRETARY OF EDUCATION, Betsy DeVos, had only just announced that she would visit Marjory Stoneman Douglas High School when the students began to react.

"Good thing I was already planning on sleeping in tomorrow," Emma González tweeted out to her 1.2 million followers Tuesday evening.

"Literally no one asked for this," said her classmate, Sarah Chadwick, to an additional 269,000 followers.

And with a handful of tweets, the students had overtaken another adult official's narrative. They were in command of their own story once again.

It has become obvious that many of the most well-known students at Stoneman Douglas in Parkland, Fla., are adept at using social media, and Twitter in particular, where many journalists spend much of their time talking to one another.

With their consistent tweeting of stories, memes, jokes and video clips, the students have managed to keep the tragedy that their school experienced — and their plan to stop such shootings from happening elsewhere — in the news for weeks, long after past mass shootings have faded from the headlines.

Many observers have simply assumed that, like fish in water, the students are skilled simply because they have been using the platforms for most of their lives. That is not entirely true.

Ms. González became one of the most well-known of the shooting survivors after giving a passionate speech about gun control the Saturday after the attack. But when her name began to trend on Twitter, she did not know how to use it.

"You know that meme where it's a picture of a grandma in front of a computer?" she said in a recent interview. "That was me. In the early days, someone DM'd me and I was like, 'O.K., so how do I respond? Where does the keyboard go?' " (A DM is a private message.)

Ms. González, 18, had been more of a Tumblr fan. She was also a fan of Instagram, but, before the shooting, had begun to use the platform less frequently after realizing she was wasting her time on it.

And Facebook?

"Facebook is not really used by the people in my community."

Ms. González was surrounded by classmates who were familiar with Twitter's ever-evolving dialect of memes, wisecracks and news stories. Within a week, she said, they had taught her the basics. How to make a thread. How to follow a thread. And, perhaps most importantly, the difference between a retweet, which reposts someone else's tweet, and a quote tweet, which allows a user to retweet with a comment above the original.

The Parkland students' use of quote tweets is one of their most effective tools. Ms. Chadwick, in particular, has used the technique, as well as other memes to mock the students' ideological opponents.

In one memorable exchange, Ms. Chadwick was scrolling through her Twitter feed last month when she saw someone remark that politicians were "easy to buy." She and her classmates had spent the last week educating themselves on how easy the AR-15 was to purchase. She made the obvious connection, and tweeted:

We should change the names of AR-15s to "Marco Rubio" because they are so easy to buy.

— Sarah Chadwick (@Sarahchadwickk) Feb. 23, 2018

The Fox News host Laura Ingraham chided Ms. Chadwick, 16, for her tone, and attributed the quote to "Stoneman Douglas sophomore Sarah Chadwick."

Ms. Chadwick's response?

I'm a junior.

— Sarah Chadwick (@Sarahchadwickk) Feb. 23, 2018

Given their single-minded focus on preventing school shootings, the more prominent Parkland students most often find themselves tangling with conservative politicians and commentators who support broad gun ownership rights, including Senator Marco Rubio, Ms. Ingraham, the N.R.A. spokeswoman Dana Loesch and the Fox News contributor Tomi Lahren.

The Florida senator, who has vast experience being mocked on Twitter by his political opponents, declined to comment directly on Ms. Chadwick's tweet. A spokeswoman for Mr. Rubio pointed toward his recent tweets about political discourse, and how the two sides need to learn to talk each other again.

In response to a call and texts, Ms. Loesch, who is usually not shy about responding online or elsewhere to critics, directed an interview request to an N.R.A. official, who declined to comment.

And as for Ms. DeVos? Students said that she spoke to few of them on her visit Wednesday, and left in a hurry.

I thought she would at least give us her "thoughts and prayers," but she refused to even meet/speak with students. I don't understand the point of her being here

— Carly Novell (@car_nove) Mar. 7, 2018

In an interview on Tuesday, Ms. Lahren applauded the students' use of social media to fight for their views. She said she was not bothered by quote tweets, which she saw as simply "a way to continue a conversation," a tool that she said that she also used frequently.

But when it was pointed out that one of Ms. Chadwick's meme tweets instructed her to "stop talking," she added: "I hope these kids understand that free speech isn't just saying what you want to say, it's hearing what you don't want to hear. It's great to be vocal about your stance but simply telling someone to stop talking doesn't seem very constructive."

Quote tweeting may allow Twitter users some small window into the other sides of a debate. Delaney Tarr, who had about 500 followers before the shooting and now has close to 97,000, said she believed the tool breaks through the filter bubbles that keep ideological opponents from hearing each other.

"Even if people maybe side with the other people a little bit more, they understand both sides," she said, of the benefits of quote tweeting. "We want people to be educated."

The social media activism has come with a cost for the high schoolers, who before the shooting just used these platforms to keep up with friends, make jokes and pass the time. Ms. Tarr was one of several students interviewed who said that she no longer felt comfortable using her Twitter account to express her opinions on pop culture, or the other lighter subjects she used to tweet about.

"The fact is that I have to represent our movement," she said. "It's not just me tweeting whatever I want to tweet about. It has to be drawn back to who I am to the media, to who I am to the country."

It is another way in which the students at Parkland have lost the normalcy of their teenage years. Ryan Deitsch said that he did not feel comfortable even tweeting his opinion of "Black Panther" (he thought it was great and that comparisons to "Thor: Ragnarok" were beside the point). Many other parts of his life have been put on hold. He has yet to respond to the colleges that have accepted him.

All of the students scoffed at the idea that they were coordinating their tweets. But they did say that as they are all following one another on the various platforms, they frequently alight on the same subject or tweet. (When reached for interviews, several of them were in the same room.) On Tuesday, a handful of them worked together to make a video parody of Ms. Loesch's own video using an hourglass to tell celebrities and other N.R.A. critics "your time is running out."

But while Ms. González and Ms. Chadwick said they usually composed their tweets on the fly, Ms. Tarr said she often took more time, mindful of her new audience and of the gravity of what she says online now.

"I'll start typing a tweet, then I'll delete it," she said. "I'll think 'what else can I say' then type and delete again. I do miss having that teenage Twitter account. But we don't get that regular teenage life anymore. It just doesn't exist."

Why Demonstrating Is Good for Kids

BY LISA DAMOUR | MARCH 12, 2018

PARTICIPATING IN POLITICAL activism may be good for our teenagers, according to a new research report.

The study, published in January in the journal Child Development, found that late adolescents and young adults who voted, volunteered or engaged in activism ultimately went further in school and had higher incomes than those who did not mobilize for political or social change.

By tracking nearly 10,000 young people from a wide variety of ethnic, racial and economic backgrounds, researchers from Wake Forest School of Medicine, Fordham University and the University of Massachusetts measured the long-term implications of youth political and social engagement. Remarkably, they found that civic activity linked to better academic and financial outcomes regardless of early school performance and parental education levels, two factors that usually drive later success.

Of course, correlation does not prove causation, but the study makes a case for the benefits of civic engagement.

In light of the findings, Parissa Ballard, the study's lead author and an assistant professor in the department of family and community medicine at Wake Forest School of Medicine, said that "having meaningful opportunities to volunteer or be involved in activism may change how young people think about themselves or their possibilities for the future."

The research is especially timely as American students consider whether to participate in the National School Walkout planned for Wednesday.

In the aftermath of the killing of 17 students and teachers in Parkland, Fla., teenagers around the country are planning to leave their school buildings on Wednesday at 10 a.m. for 17 minutes, a demonstration meant to honor the victims and advocate for gun control. Taking part in a single event — whether this one or another that matches the child's political leanings — may not, by itself, alter the trajectory of an adolescent's development. But the study's authors suggest that positive, lasting outcomes may result if organized civic engagement helps young people galvanize their belief in their personal efficacy, connect to empowering social networks or cultivate professional skills.

Indeed, the teenage survivors of the Marjory Stoneman Douglas High School shooting are already making a difference: Gov. Rick Scott of Florida credited them with inspiring new gun control legislation he signed last week.

For teenagers who intend to participate in the National School Walkout, this same study comes with an interesting caveat: Not all forms of political and social action confer equal benefits on young people. Though voting and volunteering both forecast lower levels of depression and smarter health choices down the line, activism does not.

"Activism," Dr. Ballard said, "is usually a different social experience than other forms of civic engagement." While casting ballots and serving others both enjoy broad cultural support and are reliably gratifying, "activism tends to be more controversial. Activism can be empowering. But it can also be experienced as difficult and stressful."

Indeed, the youth who engaged in activism — defined by the researchers as participating in a march or rally — enjoyed the positive benefits of greater educational attainment and larger incomes as they aged. But unlike those who only voted or volunteered, they also went on to engage in higher levels of risky health behaviors such as eating fast food, smoking cigarettes, using marijuana or binge drinking when they were between the ages of 24 and 32.

The study's authors propose two possible explanations for this.

First, activists have, historically, often been members of counter-culture groups where risk-taking may already have been the norm. Second, activists might become discouraged by the glacial pace of social change and turn to poor health habits to manage their frustration.

"We can help young people reframe their expectations from big ideas to small wins," Dr. Ballard said. "The expectation shouldn't be changing federal policy right away, but getting news coverage and raising awareness."

According to Dr. Ballard, adults can also help teenagers feel that their activism is effective by making it about connection: "connecting with others, connecting with a cause and connecting with what's already going on." While most teenagers are too young to express their opinions by voting, participating in rallies is a way to make their voices heard. Those who want to join the effort to end school shootings can look to the student-led March for Our Lives movement to learn about the global rallies scheduled for March 24 — a Saturday, so there is no conflict with classroom time.

Of course the decision about whether to support or disapprove of a teenager's activism is as personal as any in family life. Some adults will cheer on students who wish to participate in the walkout while others may oppose them or worry about the potential safety hazards, educational costs or disciplinary consequences of joining in. While some schools have threatened to suspend students who participate, legal scholars say students have the right to demonstrate unless they are disruptive. And dozens of colleges and universities said that any disciplinary actions against those participating in the protests would not affect their admissions decisions.

Looking at the issue from a social science perspective, adults should nurture adolescents' efforts to catalyze political and social change because civic engagement can help teenagers grow. America has a long history of benefiting from the activism of young people; it's good to know that the young people usually benefit, too.

LISA DAMOUR is a psychologist in Shaker Heights, Ohio, and the author of "Untangled: Guiding Teenage Girls Through the Seven Transitions Into Adulthood."

Beyond Gun Control, Student Marchers Aim to Upend Elections

BY ALEXANDER BURNS AND JULIE TURKEWITZ | MARCH 22, 2018

ON SATURDAY, Rebecca Schneid plans to pull on her sneakers, sling a camera over her shoulder and march down Pennsylvania Avenue in Washington with thousands of other students demanding an end to the gun violence that has cut through so many American communities.

But to Ms. Schneid, a survivor of the school shooting that killed 17 people last month in Parkland, Fla., the march is just the beginning — a moment of political awakening, she hopes, that will put the nation on notice that young people plan to be a greater, more organized force than teenagers and college students in the past.

"It's going to look like millions and millions of people," said Ms. Schneid, 16, who is the editor of the newspaper at Marjory Stoneman Douglas High School in Parkland. "And it's going to look scary to politicians."

With more than 800 student-led demonstrations planned in the United States and internationally, the organizers of the March for Our Lives are aiming for a generational show of strength by a diverse movement united in a conviction that adults have failed them.

Still, for all their fierce energy, these liberal-leaning activists have yet to be tested in the arena of electoral politics. They face a political system that is historically resistant to major change, and a Republican president and Congress with a strong base of support among much older voters, many of whom have more conservative views on guns.

A major moment will come in the 2018 midterm elections: Some students will be eligible to vote in November, and have vowed to make gun laws a central issue. Many more hope to organize networks and lay groundwork to vent their frustration — about pervasive school violence, and an unjust political system they view as enabling it — in the next vote for president in 2020.

David Hogg, right, a student from Marjory Stoneman Douglas High School in Parkland, Fla., spoke on Thursday to students at Thurgood Marshall Academy in Washington, D.C., about activism and Saturday's marches against gun violence.

Whether the students of the post-Parkland movement become a disruptive force depends, in large part, on if they stay organized and register to vote. There is a big practical difference between tuning into politics and actually voting, political strategists and organizers say, and young people often vote at lower rates than older ones, especially in midterm elections.

Page Gardner, president of Women's Voices Women Vote Action Fund, a Democratic-aligned group that focuses on mobilizing young people, minorities and single women, said the big question was whether teenagers' activism would translate into votes. The gun issue, she said, had become a focal point for young people who are "just fed up" with the way government works now.

"They do think the system is rigged; this is just an example of it," Ms. Gardner said of the gun issue. "They want to change it. Whether or not they register and vote to change it, is obviously the $64 million question."

The students have come of age during a time of political tumult — starting with President Trump's election and erupting in a new and more focused way with last month's school shooting. Having already reignited the political debate around guns, they believe they have the potential to bend the ideological and partisan lines of American politics more decisively as they join the electorate.

Lane Murdock, 15, a high school student in Connecticut who is organizing a wave of school-walkout protests on April 20, said the combination of the gun massacres and Mr. Trump's surprise win had jarred her out of political complacency.

"We were raised to let the adults do the work," said Ms. Murdock, who is traveling to Washington to join the march there. "When I was growing up and Obama was president, I didn't pay much attention to politics."

She called Mr. Trump's election a turning point: "I think kids are frustrated that they really couldn't have a say."

A number of the most prominent young activists from Parkland have already become familiar faces in Washington, and several arrived in the city early on Thursday to meet with students at Thurgood Marshall Academy, a school in Anacostia, a predominantly African-American neighborhood, to discuss gun violence.

Senator Chris Murphy, a Connecticut Democrat who has been meeting regularly with high school-age activists, said they stood out from other groups in their scorn for the political status quo. Mr. Murphy, who became a fierce advocate for gun control after the murder of 20 children in a 2012 mass shooting at Sandy Hook Elementary School in Newtown, Conn., said he had urged the students to dig in for a long fight, on a historic scale — "like the Civil Rights movement or the anti-Vietnam War movement."

"These kids are impatient," said Mr. Murphy, who at 44 is one of the Senate's youngest members. "This is a generation that is used to demanding immediate gratification, and they want it politically, too."

The March for Our Lives is likely to echo other mass demonstrations that have sprung up since Mr. Trump's election. Like the Women's March, it is to be anchored in Washington with speeches from students from around the country, and complemented by satellite rallies in cities and towns as large as Los Angeles and as small as Pinedale, Wyo.

The National Park Service has approved a permit for the Washington march that estimates 500,000 people could attend, which would make it one of the most impressive displays of collective political will since the last presidential election — and the only one in which many or most of the participants have never been able to vote.

Marchers like Madison Leal, however, are aching to start.

Ms. Leal, 16, a student from Stoneman Douglas, said she would hold a sign at the march bearing 17 blood-red hands and the message: "How many more?" If elected officials do not act, Ms. Leal said, "I'm going to vote them out of office."

"And so is my entire generation," she added. "And they'll be sorry then."

Among some participants, the determination to defy an indifferent political system mingles with a persistent fear of disappointment. Dantrell Blake, 21, who was shot as a teenager in Chicago and plans to march in Washington, said he hopes to draw attention to gun violence in his hometown but knows that politicians could ignore the message. The mostly black victims of gun violence in Chicago, he said, had not drawn the attention of politicians the way the Parkland shooting did.

"It's still rigged and they're still going to do what they want," Mr. Blake said of elected officials.

Those competing impulses — the drive toward political confrontation, entwined with skepticism that government will accommodate them — may come to define these students as voters. As a group, they combine liberal social beliefs with an intensely wary view of the existing political and economic order, opinion polls have found. While young people are not uniformly Democratic-leaning or supportive of gun

ERIN SCHAFF FOR THE NEW YORK TIMES

Political organizers say students in the post-Parkland movement could be a disruptive force in the coming elections — if they stay organized and register to vote. At Thurgood Marshall Academy, an audience listened Thursday to speakers at the rally against gun violence.

regulation, they are well to the left of the middle in their views. They have moved further toward Democrats since Mr. Trump's election.

Nearly three-fifths of millennial voters — a group slightly older than the high school-age marchers — identify as Democrats, according to a Pew Research Center study. That figure is much higher among women and minorities.

Conservative supporters of gun rights have watched the teen-agers' mounting activism with concern and skepticism. They have organized competing rallies this weekend in places that include Salt Lake City and Helena, Mont., but Bryan Melchior, 45, a Utah gun-rights activist, said he sees the "gun community becoming more of a minority."

Mr. Melchior, who has been organizing a march in Salt Lake City, questioned the staying power of the Parkland movement.

"It's not going to change anything about our laws," Mr. Melchior said of the march on Washington. "What I see is children that are just plain confused."

John Della Volpe, a pollster who studies young people's political views for the Harvard Kennedy School's Institute of Politics, said the gun issue was part of a larger array of social views that define the next wave of voters. While young people are largely liberal, he said they were united chiefly by their dissatisfaction with the existing political system.

"I think that's what we're seeing in this movement, in a raw form," said Mr. Della Volpe, who met this week with some of the Stoneman Douglas activists.

And at least some of the students marching this weekend have already taken steps toward becoming voters.

In Colorado, Rachel Hill, 16, a junior at Columbine High School, the site of a deadly 1999 attack, said she came from a politically mixed family but when she recently signed up to vote — under a Colorado law allowing teenagers to register early — she had identified herself as a Democrat. Ms. Hill said guns were part of the reason, but so were issues like immigration, abortion and gay and transgender rights.

Ms. Hill, who led a walkout at her school to protest gun violence this month, said she plans to march at a rally at the Colorado capitol this weekend. And her aspirations have swerved toward politics for the long term, too: while she once dreamed of becoming an author or an archaeologist, Ms. Hill now hopes to be a member of Congress or an ambassador.

"I thought, well, Trump," she said. "If he can get into politics and if he can get elected, why can't I?"

ALEXANDER BURNS reported from New York, and **JULIE TURKEWITZ** from Denver.

Can Teenagers Save America? They've Done It Before

OPINION | BY JON GRINSPAN | MARCH 26, 2018

WHILE MILLIONS OF Americans found this weekend's nationwide marches for gun control inspiring, many others are giving them a skeptical eye — and not just Second Amendment advocates. How could a bunch of teenagers have the wherewithal to make change in America's deadlocked politics? After all, they're just kids.

Older people have long grumbled about the young in politics, dismissing them as "baby politicians" or "beardless boys" in the early years of this country. But when American politics were at their darkest, in the late 19th century, it was young people who broke a partisan divide and helped save democracy. Maybe they can do it again.

Democracy, as a rule, has a labor problem. Someone has to do the hard, unpaid work of persuading millions of citizens to participate. For much of our history, enthusiastic young people did that labor for free. Even today, visit any campaign headquarters and you will find a sea of youthful volunteers phone-banking and poster-making. But while young people have long done an outsize portion of the political work, they were rarely allowed to pick the issues politics addressed.

It was only when adult politicians seemed stalled and issueless that a generation of young people stepped up to lead.

For much of the first century of American politics, young people operated as unpaid foot soldiers of partisan political armies. In a popular, loud, dirty system there was plenty of unglamorous work to be done. For every enormous rally or rowdy election, there were people still too young to vote working behind the scenes, handing out ballots and emptying spittoons, toasting allies' speeches and cracking rivals' skulls.

The one thing young people were not supposed to do, for much of the 1800s, was to champion themselves. They were referred to as "generous and unsophisticated" — worker bees to be directed by the older and wiser. As one 16-year-old antislavery activist in Maine complained, when he tried to talk politics with voters many laughed at his "childish enthusiasm and coolly reminded me that I was a boy."

Even among youthful activists, many felt conflicted about whether they should "originate opinions" or merely carry them out. Young men and women were raised to revere their democracy, did they really have a right to guide it yet? During an 1831 rally against what they called the "slimy mark" President Andrew Jackson was leaving on the country, young men in Baltimore nonetheless worried that they were "overstepping the modesty which befits our age."

When young men and women did play a role in their nation's politics, it was often over the resistance of older Americans. When young African-Americans in Philadelphia in 1838 fought to keep black Pennsylvanians' right to vote, they had to justify themselves even to their own community. Dismissed as "inexperienced, hasty, immature" by their elders, young black Philadelphians published newspaper statements directed at the city's black elite, announcing "*we will not be put down.*"

This was an age that could not afford to "put down" the young. Over the second half of the 1800s, American politics darkened. The succession of Civil War, Reconstruction and the Gilded Age was marked by bitter partisanship, endemic corruption, appalling violence and a general sense that democracy was failing. Adults seemed to be stuck, recycling the same partisan issues over and over.

And they insisted that the young follow their lead. As an established Minnesota politico told one rising 25-year-old: Don't think, just follow the party's platform, just "swallow it down."

But in the final years of the 19th century, a sudden burst of young people demanded new issues — their issues. Tired of, as one Coloradan put it, "rotten old hulks who monopolize the offices and dwell upon the past," a generation of young men and women denounced their leaders and with them, partisanship. They demanded political reform, labor reform and social reform, and declared that they would withhold their votes from any party that didn't respond. "The ratio of party feeling and self-interest is rapidly changing," declared one sharp-tongued New Yorker in 1898, adding that "the younger generation hates both parties equally."

Politicians saw the change and chased after those young voters. Soon, The Washington Post was begging: "Don't sneer at them as 'boys,' when they drop into your ward meetings, don't make them do all the work of the campaign."

In the new century, young people's "self interest" helped kill extreme polarization by forcing both parties to pursue the same set of demands. Youthful independent voters emerged as a decisive third force, with just enough influence to swing close elections. Politicians scrambled after them, beginning the Progressive Era, passing laws protecting workers, cleaning up cities and championing the young.

Women played a key role in this shift. Because they could not vote, they were less corrupted by partisanship. Women in their 20s worked to refocus American public life toward social concerns. They built schools — nearly one a day between 1890 and 1920 — and fought child labor. The aggressive crusader Florence Kelley wrote that protecting young people is "the noblest duty of the Republic," an act of "self preservation" that enables the next generation to champion itself.

This is the key to understanding youth politics. Young people cannot be truly selfish, because they cannot be permanently young. Youth is temporary, its gains are passed on. In the late 19th century, young people built institutions that helped protect 20th-century young people. The high school seniors marching over the weekend will hopefully make their schools safer well after they have graduated. If anyone should be choosing the issues in politics, it should be the young, for they "have a longer future to provide for."

JON GRINSPAN, a historian at the Smithsonian's National Museum of American History, is the author of "The Virgin Vote: How Young Americans Made Democracy Social, Politics Personal and Voting Popular in the Nineteenth Century."

Are Today's Teenagers Smarter and Better Than We Think?

BY TARA PARKER-POPE | MARCH 30, 2018

TODAY'S TEENAGERS HAVE been raised on cellphones and social media. Should we worry about them or just get out of their way?

A recent wave of student protests around the country has provided a close-up view of Generation Z in action, and many adults have been surprised. While there has been much hand-wringing about this cohort, also called iGen or the Post-Millennials, the stereotype of a disengaged, entitled and social-media-addicted generation doesn't match the poised, media-savvy and inclusive young people leading the protests and gracing magazine covers.

There's 18-year-old Emma González, whose shaved head, impassioned speeches and torn jeans have made her the iconic face of the #NeverAgain movement, which developed after the 17 shooting deaths in February at Marjory Stoneman Douglas High School in Parkland, Fla. Naomi Wadler, just 11, became an overnight sensation after confidently telling a national television audience she represented "African-American girls whose stories don't make the front page of every national newspaper." David Hogg, a high school senior at Stoneman Douglas, has weathered numerous personal attacks with the disciplined calm of a seasoned politician.

Sure, these kids could be outliers. But plenty of adolescent researchers believe they are not.

"I think we must contemplate that technology is having the exact opposite effect than we perceived," said Julie Lythcott-Haims, the former dean of freshmen at Stanford University and author of "How to Raise an Adult." "We see the negatives of not going outside, can't look people in the eye, don't have to go through the effort of making a phone call. There are ways we see the deficiencies that social media has offered, but there are obviously tremendous upsides and positives as well."

"I am fascinated by the phenomenon we are seeing in front of us, and I don't think it's unique to these six or seven kids who have been the face of the Parkland adolescent cohort," says Lisa Damour, an adolescent psychologist and author of "Untangled: Guiding Teenage Girls Through the Seven Transitions Into Adulthood."

"They are so direct in their messaging. They are so clear. They seem unflappable."

Dr. Damour, who has spent her career talking and listening to teenagers, said she believes the Parkland teens are showing the world the potential of their peer group. "Those of us who live with teenagers and are around them can see something that is different about this generation," she said.

There is still much to learn about the postmillennial cohort — social scientists haven't even agreed on when this generation begins, although there seems to be a consensus forming that the year 2000, give or take a few years, is a good place to start. But data collected from various health surveys already show that today's teens are different from previous generations in many ways.

Many risky behaviors have dropped sharply among today's teens. Cigarette smoking among teens is at a historic low since peaking in the mid 1990s. Alcohol use has also declined significantly — the number of teens who have used alcohol in the past 30 days is down by half since the 1990s. Teen pregnancy rates have hit historic lows, and teens over all are waiting longer to have sex than their parent's generation. Teen driving fatalities are down about 64 percent since 1975. Some of that is attributed to safer cars, but teen crashes have declined between 10 and 30 percent in states with tiered licensing systems, and teen drunken driving has dropped while teen seatbelt use has increased.

While most health researchers celebrate these changes in teen health, some scientists think the trends suggest a lower level of maturity among today's teens. Perhaps teens are safer simply because their reliance on social media and smartphone use means they are getting out less. In September, the journal Child Development published a study by Jean Twenge, a psychology professor at San Diego State University, noting that there is a decline in a number of "adult" activities among today's teens. In seven large, nationally representative surveys of eight million American adolescents from 1976 to 2016, fewer adolescents in recent years are having sex, dating, drinking alcohol, driving, working for pay and going out without their parents.

"The big picture is that they are taking longer to grow up," said Dr. Twenge, whose latest book is "iGen: Why Today's Super-Connected Kids Are Growing Up Less Rebellious, More Tolerant, Less Happy — and Completely Unprepared for Adulthood."

In an article in The Atlantic last fall titled "Have Smartphones Destroyed a Generation?," Dr. Twenge argued that teens are more comfortable in their bedrooms or on smartphones or social media than at a party. While they are physically safer than past generations as a result, rates of teen depression and suicide are on the rise. "It's not an exaggeration to describe iGen as being on the brink of the worst mental-health crisis in decades," she wrote. "Much of this deterioration can be traced to their phones."

But a number of social scientists and adolescent health researchers disagree with that conclusion. While teen depression and suicide rates are worrisome, there is no causal link to show those trends are the result of smartphones and social media. In fact, a literature review by Unicef researchers in December found that moderate use of digital technology tends to be beneficial for children's mental well-being, while no use or too much use is associated with a "small negative impact." The larger issues that affect a child's well-being are family functioning, social dynamics at school and socio-economic conditions, the report concluded.

Don Tapscott, author of "Grown Up Digital," said he believes today's teenagers are better communicators than any previous generation. "They didn't grow up being the passive recipients of somebody else's broadcast," he said. "They grew up being interactors and communicators. In the 1960s we had a generation gap. What we have today is a generation lap — they are lapping their parents on the digital track."

The clinical psychologist Wendy Mogel interviewed groups of middle school and high school students around the country in 2015 and 2016 for her new book, "Voice Lessons for Parents: What to Say, How to Say It and When to Listen." Dr. Mogel spoke with diverse kids from various regions and walks of life, but found herself consistently impressed by their thoughtfulness, how much they liked their parents, and how much they cared about the world around them.

"The press and general public like to see them as spoiled and not having to work hard for anything except grades and being very entitled," Dr. Mogel said. "But they're courageous, energetic, optimistic and really smart."

Neil Howe, a historian whose books include "Millennials Rising," said that unlike earlier generations, today's teens have accepted the structures of society and have learned to work within those boundaries. "They're very good at using rules to make their point, and they're absolutely excellent at negotiating with their parents, and negotiating in a reasonable way about how to bend these rules in a way that will make them more effective and give them more space," he said. "This is not a 'throw the brick through the window and burn stuff down' group of kids at all. They're working very constructively, arm-in-arm with older people they trust, to make big institutions work better and make them stronger and more effective."

Ms. Lythcott-Haims notes that the current crop of teenagers is the first generation to grow up with active shooter drills since kindergarten. "I think what we might have here is a generation that really defines itself by the markers of their childhoods," she said. "In addition to being marked by these gun violence tragedies, they came to consciousness with a black man in the White House and smartphones in their hands."

What does all this mean for the future of today's teens? All of the researchers agreed there is still much more to learn about this cohort, but what we know so far is promising.

"We are in the process of distilling the data and discerning who they are, but I am excited," said Ms. Lythcott-Haims. "We don't know who they will be in their 20s, but already they have agency, the sense of your own existence, your own right to make decisions and your own responsibility for outcomes and consequences. That's what we need to have to be mentally well. I think these folks could turn out not to be just leaders, but to be a generation that we look back on and end up calling one of the greatest."

Maybe Girls Will Save Us

OPINION | BY RESHMA SAUJANI | OCT. 10, 2018

They've eclipsed boys in political participation and shown incredible moral clarity.

AS CHRISTINE BLASEY FORD testified before the Senate Judiciary Committee last month, women across the country took to the streets and social media in support of her and sexual assault survivors around the world.

Two of them were teenage girls — seniors at the high school Dr. Blasey attended in the 1980s — who shared a ticket to the hearing, silently alternating in and out of a seat at the back of the hearing room. It was a show of solidarity that spoke volumes about the moment we're living in. Those two teenagers are part of a generation of girls who've been at the helm of some of the most transformative social movements in recent memory.

Take a look at this list, and you'll see what I mean:

Emma González, a graduate of Marjory Stoneman Douglas High School, and Naomi Wadler, who organized a walkout of her Virginia elementary school, made headlines as advocates for gun control at ages 18 and 11. The Olympic gymnast Aly Raisman became a force in the #MeToo movement at 23, when she revealed that she had been abused by the team doctor.

As a sixth grader, Marley Dias started a campaign to promote and share books featuring black girls. Mari Copeny has been the face of the fight for clean water in Flint, Mich., since she was 8. Sophie Cruz was just 6 when she spoke at the Women's March about immigration reform. Jasilyn Charger, at 21, coordinated a 2,000-mile run from North Dakota to Washington to raise awareness about the impact of the Dakota Access Pipeline on Standing Rock.

And beyond these headline-grabbing female activists is an entire cohort — whether you call them Gen Z or post-millennials or simply

DORIS LIOU

"young" — who seem to have eclipsed their male counterparts in political participation.

According to a January report by the nonpartisan opinion research organization PRRI, 48 percent of 15- to 24-year-old women say they have signed an online petition, compared to only 39 percent of men in the same age group. They were 23 percent more likely to say they had volunteered for a group or cause they cared about and 39 percent more likely to say they had donated money to a campaign or a cause.

Why are today's girls — many of whom are so young that it will be years before they're able to cast ballots — taking to the streets and to social media calling for change?

Here's something that might explain it: More than ever, they have plentiful, visible, diverse role models. Since the huge women's marches that followed Donald Trump's inauguration, there's been no shortage of high-profile political action by women. According to an April report by Pew Research Center, almost a third of women ages 18 to 49 had attended a political event or protest since the 2016 election. It's no wonder some have argued that 2018, like 1992, should be called "The Year of the Woman." In July, 58 percent of women surveyed said they had been paying increased attention to politics since Mr. Trump's election, compared with 46 percent of men. A record number of women, 476, filed to run this year for the House of Representatives.

When I think of the effect these politically active women are having on the younger generation, I'm reminded of one of the mantras at my organization, Girls Who Code, which is dedicated to closing the gender gap in technology: Girls cannot be what they cannot see. We know that without role models who look like them in computer science, they're unlikely to even consider the field. A recent study, "Who Becomes an Inventor in America? The Importance of Exposure to Innovation," estimated that if girls were as exposed to female inventors as much as boys are to male inventors, female innovation rates would rise by 164 percent and the gender gap in innovation would fall by more than half.

In the same way that female innovators beget innovation by girls, the high-profile political activism of women this year might explain increased engagement among our girls. As a 2006 study by University of Notre Dame researchers concluded, "The more politics is infused with visible female role models, the more adolescent girls report an expectation of being involved in politics."

Beyond simply being involved, the girls of this generation are as passionate and unapologetic about what matters to them as any in history. They display a sense of moral clarity, an instinct for inclusiveness, and a commitment to making the world a better place for people of all ages and genders. The rest of us should follow their lead.

RESHMA SAUJANI is the founder and chief executive of Girls Who Code.

Glossary

A.C.L.U. The American Civil Liberties Union, a nonprofit organization that works to protect individual rights and liberties granted by the Constitution.

activist A person who fights for social or political change.

ad hominem An argument, attack or reaction toward a person instead of the position they are holding.

advocate A person who publicly speaks for a cause.

ally Someone who supports or helps another person, organization or cause.

AR-15 A semiautomatic rifle in the style of the ArmaLite rifle, a company that developed it in the 1950s. This weapon is commonly used in mass shootings and is a source of controversy in the gun-control debate.

assault weapons A term used to describe some firearms, usually including automatic and semiautomatic weapons.

cadet A trainee in the armed services or police force.

die-in A style of demonstration in which participants lie down as if dead.

gun control Laws and policies that regulate the manufacturing, sale and ownership of guns.

legislator A person who makes laws.

March for Our Lives A student-led march for stricter gun control laws.

mass shooting A shooting in which multiple people are injured or killed. The legal definition is not precise on how many injuries or casualties qualify a mass shooting, leading to discrepancies and unclarity around the frequency of such incidents.

movement In terms of activism, a type of group action.

Newtown The city of the Sandy Hook Elementary School shooting, in which a gunman killed 20 elementary school children and six adult staff members.

N.R.A. The National Rifle Association, a gun rights advocacy group.

Parkland The city in which the Marjory Stoneman Douglas High School shooting took place.

plaintiff A person who brings a legal case against, or sues, someone in court.

R.O.T.C. The Reserve Officers' Training Corps, which trains and prepares young adults for the U.S. military.

Second Amendment The amendment to the Bill of Rights used to defend individual rights to bear arms.

Media Literacy Terms

"Media literacy" refers to the ability to access, understand, critically assess and create media. The following terms are important components of media literacy, and they will help you critically engage with the articles in this title.

angle The aspect of a news story that a journalist focuses on and develops.

attribution The method by which a source is identified or by which facts and information are assigned to the person who provided them.

balance Principle of journalism that both perspectives of an argument should be presented in a fair way.

commentary A type of story that is an expression of opinion on recent events by a journalist generally known as a commentator.

credibility The quality of being trustworthy and believable, said of a journalistic source.

critical review A type of story that describes an event or work of art, such as a theater performance, film, concert, book, restaurant, radio or television program, exhibition or musical piece, and offers critical assessment of its quality and reception.

editorial Article of opinion or interpretation.

fake news A fictional or made-up story presented in the style of a legitimate news story, intended to deceive readers; also commonly used to criticize legitimate news that one dislikes because of its perspective or unfavorable coverage of a subject.

feature story Article designed to entertain as well as to inform.

human interest story A type of story that focuses on individuals and how events or issues affect their lives, generally offering a sense of relatability to the reader.

impartiality Principle of journalism that a story should not reflect a journalist's bias and should contain balance.

intention The motive or reason behind something, such as the publication of a news story.

interview story A type of story in which the facts are gathered primarily by interviewing another person or persons.

news story An article or style of expository writing that reports news, generally in a straightforward fashion and without editorial comment.

op-ed An opinion piece that reflects a prominent individual's opinion on a topic of interest.

paraphrase The summary of an individual's words, with attribution, rather than a direct quotation of their exact words.

quotation The use of an individual's exact words indicated by the use of quotation marks and proper attribution.

reliability The quality of being dependable and accurate, said of a journalistic source.

rhetorical device Technique in writing intending to persuade the reader or communicate a message from a certain perspective.

source The origin of the information reported in journalism.

style A distinctive use of language in writing or speech; also a news or publishing organization's rules for consistent use of language with regard to spelling, punctuation, typography and capitalization, usually regimented by a house style guide.

tone A manner of expression in writing or speech.

Media Literacy Questions

1. Identify the various sources cited in the article "Reaching Out to Younger Hearts and Minds About L.G.B.T.Q. People" (on page 21). How does Scott James attribute information to each of these sources in the article? How effective are James's attributions in helping the reader identify his sources?

2. Often, as a news story develops, a journalist's attitude toward the subject may change. Compare "In Novel Tactic on Climate Change, Citizens Sue Their Governments" (on page 52) and "Young People Are Suing the Trump Administration Over Climate Change. She's Their Lawyer." (on page 69), both by John Schwartz. Did new information discovered between the publication of these two articles change Schwartz's perspective?

3. What type of story is "Meet the Teenagers Leading a Climate Change Movement" (on page 58)? Can you identify another article in this collection that is the same type of story? What elements helped you come to your conclusion?

4. Compare the headlines of "Students Lead Huge Rallies for Gun Control Across the U.S." (on page 100) and "For Parkland Students, a Surreal Journey From 'Normal' to a Worldwide March" (on page 106). Which is a more compelling headline, and why? How could the less compelling headline be changed to better draw the reader's interest?

5. What is the intention of the article "At Rallies, Students With a Different View of Gun Violence: As Urban Reality" (on page 123)? How effectively does it achieve its intended purpose?

6. Analyze the authors' reporting in "The View From Opposite Sides of a Student Walkout in Montana" (on page 131) and "What Three Days With the Parkland Student Activists Taught Me" (on page 174). Do you think one journalist is more balanced in her reporting than the other? If so, why do you think so?

7. " 'Let Us Have a Childhood': On the Road With the Parkland Activists" (on page 162) features photographs. What do these photographs add to the article?

8. What type of story is "Why Demonstrating Is Good for Kids" (on page 192)? Can you identify another article in this collection that is the same type of story? What elements helped you come to your conclusion?

9. Does "Beyond Gun Control, Student Marchers Aim to Upend Elections" (on page 195) use multiple sources? What are the strengths of using multiple sources in a journalistic piece? What are the weaknesses of relying heavily on only one or a few sources?

10. What is the intention of the article "Are Today's Teenagers Smarter and Better Than We Think?" (on page 204)? How effectively does it achieve its intended purpose?

11. The article "Maybe Girls Will Save Us" (on page 209) is an example of an op-ed. Identify how Reshma Saujani's attitude and tone help convey her opinion on the topic.

Citations

All citations in this list are formatted according to the
Modern Language Association's (MLA) style guide.

BOOK CITATION

THE NEW YORK TIMES EDITORIAL STAFF. *Teen Activists*. New York: New York
  Times Educational Publishing, 2020.

ONLINE ARTICLE CITATIONS

ARANGO, TIM, AND MATT STEVENS. "The East L.A. Walkouts, 50 Years Later."
  The New York Times, 6 Mar. 2018, https://www.nytimes.com/2018/03/06
  /us/california-today-east-la-student-walkouts.html.

ASTOR, MAGGIE. " 'Let Us Have a Childhood': On the Road With the Parkland
  Activists." *The New York Times*, 15 Aug. 2018, www.nytimes.com/2018/08
  /15/us/politics/parkland-students-voting.html.

ASTOR, MAGGIE. "What Three Days With the Parkland Student Activists
  Taught Me." *The New York Times*, 16 Aug. 2018, www.nytimes.com/2018
  /08/16/insider/parkland-student-activists-tour.html.

BAKER, AL. "Baring Shoulders and Knees, Students Protest a Dress Code."
  The New York Times, 6 June 2012, www.nytimes.com/2012/06/07/nyregion
  /stuyvesant-high-school-students-protest-dress-code.html.

BROMWICH, JONAH ENGEL. "How the Parkland Students Got So Good at Social
  Media." *The New York Times*, 7 Mar. 2018, www.nytimes.com/2018/03/07
  /us/parkland-students-social-media.html.

BROMWICH, JONAH ENGEL. "Parkland Students Find Themselves Targets
  of Lies and Personal Attacks." *The New York Times*, 27 Mar. 2018, www
  .nytimes.com/2018/03/27/us/parkland-students-hogg-gonzalez.html.

BURCH, AUDRA D. S. "Parkland Activist Got Some College Rejections. He'll
  Major in 'Changing the World.' " *The New York Times*, 29 Mar. 2018, www
  .nytimes.com/2018/03/29/us/parkland-students-college-admission.html.

BURNS, ALEXANDER, AND JULIE TURKEWITZ. "Beyond Gun Control, Student Marchers Aim to Upend Elections." *The New York Times*, 22 Mar. 2018, www.nytimes.com/2018/03/22/us/politics/march-for-our-lives-gun-control.html.

CHOKSHI, NIRAJ. "2 Texas Students Sue Schools to Freely Protest the Pledge." *The New York Times*, 30 Oct. 2017, www.nytimes.com/2017/10/30/us/student-pledge-protest.html.

DAMOUR, LISA. "Why Demonstrating Is Good for Kids." *The New York Times*, 12 Mar. 2018, www.nytimes.com/2018/03/12/well/family/why-demonstrating-is-good-for-kids.html.

GOLDSTEIN, DANA. "Are Civics Lessons a Constitutional Right? This Student Is Suing for Them." *The New York Times*, 28 Nov. 2018, www.nytimes.com/2018/11/28/us/civics-rhode-island-schools.html.

GRINSPAN, JON. "Can Teenagers Save America? They've Done It Before." *The New York Times*, 28 Mar. 2018, www.nytimes.com/2018/03/26/opinion/teenagers-gun-rally.html.

HANCHETT, DAKOTA. "Why I Didn't Join My School's Walkout." *The New York Times*, 19 Mar. 2018, www.nytimes.com/2018/03/19/opinion/teenagers-guns-protests.html.

HEALY, JACK. " 'Almost No One Agrees With Us': For Rural Students, Gun Control Can Be a Lonely Cause." *The New York Times*, 22 May 2018, www.nytimes.com/2018/05/22/us/marshall-county-kentucky-student-gun-protests.html.

HUSSEY, KRISTIN. "Emboldened by Parkland, Newtown Students Find Their Voice." *The New York Times*, 26 Aug. 2018, www.nytimes.com/2018/08/26/nyregion/newtown-students-activism-parkland.html.

JAMES, SCOTT. "Reaching Out to Younger Hearts and Minds About L.G.B.T.Q. People." *The New York Times*, 19 June 2018, https://www.nytimes.com/2018/06/19/arts/lgbtq-literature-teens-and-younger.html.

KANTOR, JODI. "Malala Yousafzai, Youngest Nobel Peace Prize Winner, Adds to Her Achievements and Expectations." *The New York Times*, 10 Oct. 2014, https://www.nytimes.com/2014/10/11/world/asia/malala-yousafzai-youngest-nobel-peace-prize-winner-adds-to-her-achievements-and-expectations.html.

MARIKAR, SHEILA. " 'Where My Activists At?' Inside the First Teen Vogue Summit." *The New York Times*, 5 Dec. 2017, www.nytimes.com/2017/12/05/style/teen-vogue-summit-hillary-clinton.html.

MAZZEI, PATRICIA. "For Parkland Students, a Surreal Journey From 'Normal' to a Worldwide March." *The New York Times*, 24 Mar. 2018, www.nytimes.com/2018/03/24/us/parkland-students-gun-violence.html.

THE NEW YORK TIMES. "March for Our Lives Highlights: Students Protesting Guns Say 'Enough Is Enough.' " *The New York Times*, 24 Mar. 2018, https://www.nytimes.com/2018/03/24/us/march-for-our-lives.html.

PARKER-POPE, TARA. "Are Today's Teenagers Smarter and Better Than We Think?" *The New York Times*, 30 Mar. 2018, www.nytimes.com/2018/03/30/well/family/teenagers-generation-stoneman-douglas-parkland-.html.

SAFRONOVA, VALERIYA, AND JOANNA NIKAS. "High School Students Explain Why They Protest Anthems and Pledges." *The New York Times*, 21 Oct. 2017, https://www.nytimes.com/2017/10/21/style/high-school-students-explain-why-they-protest-anthems-and-pledges.html.

SAUJANI, RESHMA. "Maybe Girls Will Save Us." *The New York Times*, 18 Oct. 2018, www.nytimes.com/2018/10/10/opinion/maybe-girls-will-save-us.html.

SCHWARTZ, JOHN. "In Novel Tactic on Climate Change, Citizens Sue Their Governments." *The New York Times*, 10 May 2016, www.nytimes.com/2016/05/11/science/climate-change-citizen-lawsuits.html.

SCHWARTZ, JOHN. "Young People Are Suing the Trump Administration Over Climate Change. She's Their Lawyer." *The New York Times*, 23 Oct. 2018, https://www.nytimes.com/2018/10/23/climate/kids-climate-lawsuit-lawyer.html.

SHEAR, MICHAEL D. "Students Lead Huge Rallies for Gun Control Across the U.S." *The New York Times*, 24 Mar. 2018, www.nytimes.com/2018/03/24/us/politics/students-lead-huge-rallies-for-gun-control-across-the-us.html.

STEVENS, MATT. " 'Skinhead Lesbian' Tweet About Parkland Student Ends Maine Republican's Candidacy." *The New York Times*, 18 Mar. 2018, www.nytimes.com/2018/03/18/us/politics/maine-republican-leslie-gibson.html.

STEVENS, MATT. "Transgender Student in Bathroom Wins Court Ruling." *The New York Times*, 22 May 2018, https://www.nytimes.com/2018/05/22/us/gavin-grimm-transgender-bathrooms.html.

TURKEWITZ, JULIE. "The View From Opposite Sides of a Student Walkout in Montana." *The New York Times*, 15 Mar. 2018, www.nytimes.com/2018/03/15/us/school-walkout-montana.html.

TURKEWITZ, JULIE, AND ANEMONA HARTOCOLLIS. "Highlights: Students Call for Action Across Nation; Florida Lawmakers Fail to Take Up Assault Rifle Bill." *The New York Times*, 20 Feb. 2018, www.nytimes.com/2018/02/20/us/gun-control-florida-shooting.html.

TURKEWITZ, JULIE, ET AL. "Emma González Leads a Student Outcry on Guns: 'This Is the Way I Have to Grieve.'" *The New York Times*, 18 Feb. 2018, www.nytimes.com/2018/02/18/us/emma-gonzalez-florida-shooting.html.

UGWU, REGGIE. "The Education of Amandla Stenberg." *The New York Times*, 11 Sept. 2018, https://www.nytimes.com/2018/09/11/movies/amandla-stenberg-the-hate-u-give.html.

VICTOR, DANIEL. "Malala Yousafzai, Girls' Education Advocate, Finishes High School." *The New York Times*, 7 July 2017, https://www.nytimes.com/2017/07/07/world/middleeast/malala-yousafzai-graduates.html.

VICTOR, DANIEL, AND MATTHEW HAAG. " 'Swatting' Prank Sends Police to Home of David Hogg, Parkland Survivor." *The New York Times*, 5 June 2018, www.nytimes.com/2018/06/05/us/david-hogg-swatting.html.

WEILAND, NOAH. "At Rallies, Students With a Different View of Gun Violence: As Urban Reality." *The New York Times*, 24 Mar. 2018, https://www.nytimes.com/2018/03/24/us/gun-rally-urban.html.

WORKMAN, KAREN. "Missouri Teenagers Protest a Transgender Student's Use of the Girls' Bathroom." *The New York Times*, 1 Sept. 2015, www.nytimes.com/2015/09/02/us/teenagers-protest-a-transgender-students-use-of-the-girls-bathroom.html.

YEE, VIVIAN, AND ALAN BLINDER. "National School Walkout: Thousands Protest Against Gun Violence Across the U.S." *The New York Times*, 14 Mar. 2018, https://www.nytimes.com/2018/03/14/us/school-walkout.html.

YOON-HENDRICKS, ALEXANDRA. "Meet the Teenagers Leading a Climate Change Movement." *The New York Times*, 21 July 2018, www.nytimes.com/2018/07/21/us/politics/zero-hour-climate-march.html.

Index

This book is current up until the time of printing. For the most up-to-date reporting, visit www.nytimes.com.